THE MOST IMPORTANT THING TO FOCUS ON IS PURPOSE AND THIS IS YOUR DEFINITIVE PLAYBOOK

First printing 2024

Book cover designed by Burtch Hunter

Book interior designed by Carolyn Asman, Andrew Vogel, and Nicole Wedekind

ISBN 979-8-9913870-0-2 Paperback
ISBN 979-8-9913870-1-9 Hardback
ISBN 979-8-9913870-2-6 E-book

Published by Ripples Media

ripples.media

"Some men see things as they are and say why. I dream things that never were and say why not."

—*Bobby Kennedy*

DEDICATION

Jeff

As I write these books to attempt to fulfill my Purpose, I thought it appropriate to dedicate this book to someone in my life that did the same: Kemie Nix, who did so much to help others and asked for nothing in return. We love you, and we miss you.

Teresa

Dedicated to my daughter, Ace. Through the support of family and friends, I found my Purpose: "Serve and teach others so they can go on to do great things." This book is the next step in my journey. Your achievements, Ace, fill me with pride and I am eager to support your future "great things."

Megan

Dedicated to my parents: Dad for always reinforcing the power of a positive mental attitude (P.M.A.!!) and for being my greatest supporter. And Mom, for your "Squad Mom" dedication to getting me to my various school and community events that taught me teamwork and accountability. All roads that have led me to my own Purpose have been laid because of the Values you both have instilled in me.

CONTENTS

OVERVIEW

Why write this book, and who is this book for?

Maybe the better question is, why is there a section in a book that you already have in your hands describing who this book is for? After all, one of my favorite business lessons – and something I've told my children hundreds of times – is: "Don't sell past the sale."

Meaning, once you have the sale, get out of there! After the sale is made, the only thing you can do by continuing to "sell" is change the person's mind.

For example: on a Saturday afternoon recently, my daughter asked me if she could go over to her friend's house for a few hours. "Yes," I said more quickly than I probably should, but let's face it, I'm just happy she has friends in walkable distance and that she is willing to, you know, use her actual legs to walk. My son, on the other hand, won't go anywhere unless he's driven (which drives me mad . . . pun intended).

So I gave her a quick "yes" and looked back down at the book I was reading, thinking we were done with the conversation. She then proceeds to tell me that her friend is also having some boys over, and her parents aren't home, but it's cool because . . . *wait, what now? Uh, sorry honey, you're going to have to check with your mom on this one, I'm taking my "yes" back. And by the way, don't you have youth group in an hour? Should have stopped after you made the sale.*

And yet here I am, presumably already having made "the sale," but properly going against my own advice and telling you who this book is for, risking the chance that you change your mind and decide that no, this book is actually not for you after all.

But I'm betting it is.

—

It's taken me four books to realize what my readers actually really want from me. You've been telling me all along, and I've kinda listened but also kinda just written the books I wanted to write at the time.

In 2019, I published my first book (*The 5-Day Turnaround*). That book was my attempt to help non-entrepreneurs think like entrepreneurs. And seemingly every time I spoke to someone who read it, or I gave a talk on the topic, I was asked the same thing: "Hey, you know that PVTV (Purpose, Vision, Tenets, & Values) thing in the book? I'd love to learn more about that."

So, being the smart and attentive author I am, in 2020, I decided to write my next book about, you guessed it . . . leading during a crisis (*The Crisis Turnaround*). To be fair, I put some more PVTV stuff in that book, but not much more.

Again, people who read that book asked me the same question:

"Can we get some more details on that PVTV thing? Sounds pretty interesting."

I swear I've been told that I'm a good listener, by more than one person, but again I heard these questions and promptly wrote my next book in 2021, focused on . . . leading a small team *(The Great Team Turnaround)*. And again, I put more PVTV content in that book and again, it wasn't enough for people.

Deciding that despite what I had heard, what people were *really* asking me was how I've had success building great cultures at my companies (I promise I'm not normally this dense), I wrote my fourth book, *The Culture Turnaround*, in 2022. PVTV was about one-fifth of the content of that book.

I spent 2023 – the first year I missed writing a book since I started back in 2019 – thinking to myself, *what in the world should I write about next?* Hmmmm, I wonder . . .

Of course, I knew the answer. After four years of hearing the same thing over and over, I finally decided to write the definitive book on PVTV. Only now has it matured into a much broader concept: *The Purpose Playbook*.

The Purpose Playbook is the methodology that I've developed, along with a slew of people over the years (some of whom are Dragons, and two of which are my coauthors of this book: Megan Barney and Teresa Caro). This methodology helps a company or team rally around a common Purpose, shared Values, combined with a Vision for where to take the company, and the Tenets to get there, including the prep needed to start the journey as well as the strategies and tactics to ensure you stay on the right track.

So, back to the original question.

Who is this book for?

A new leader of a new team or organization who wants to create a high-performance culture.

Any leader of any team or organization who wants to be a more inspiring and capable leader.

Anyone who feels unfulfilled in their career but isn't sure why, or how to get back on track.

A team member who believes their team could be *so much better* if it just had the right leadership.

People who feel like Mondays are the worst . . . or have heard a team member say this.

An organization leader who wants to create a teamwork-centric culture, so even ad hoc teams (people who come together for a period of time and then disband) can be successful.

Any of my, Megan's, or Teresa's friends who want to support us. Kidding. Kinda.

Anyone who feels like they are in a career mid-life crisis.

Any leader who's been asked the question, "But, why?"

Any team that has trouble harnessing the incredible, combined talent of all team members.

Any young person who wants to be great at what they end up doing for their career, and knows the only way that will happen is if they're on the right kind of team (clear Purpose, clear Vision, clear objectives, clear roles, and trust of one another).

Now that you know why I (and Megan and Teresa) wrote this book, and who it was written for, I hope you're convinced that you made the right decision in purchasing it, and you're ready to dive in. Otherwise, I thoroughly screwed up by, once again, selling past the sale.

Let's get into it.

Jeff

WHAT TO EXPECT

This book is the beginning of *The Purpose Playbook*, focused on helping you develop your team's PVTV (Purpose, Vision, Tenets, & Values). While we first considered including the entire process – the development and execution of PVTV – into one book, we ultimately decided that it would benefit readers and users to split the guidance into two parts.

Developing your team's PVTV is no easy task. It takes time, patience, and a trusting leadership team (which we included in this book). You'll work with your team over many sessions and through various exercises and activities to develop an authentic and team-supported PVTV statement. We believe that effort is more than enough for one book.

We also believe there should be a period between the development of your PVTV and its active implementation and execution. This is not to say there aren't immediate steps you should take to continue the excitement that naturally comes from this process. We have included a list of activities to do this.

Executing your PVTV happens over time and is a never-ending effort to continue ensuring your team is moving in the right direction. We believe this is best handled in an additional, comprehensive book focused exclusively on the execution of PVTV.

THE TURNAROUND
LITERARY UNIVERSE

If you've read any of my previous four books, you know they all exist in the same "universe." Much the same way that the Marvel Cinematic Universe (or, the MCU for those "in the know") exists for Marvel films, I got to the point where I needed a name for this world that I've created, with characters such as Will (the agency entrepreneur who sounds an awful lot like me but I swear he's not), Charles (the dutiful and wise mentor), Rachel (the up and coming CEO), Shera (the tech startup CEO), Megan (Shera's trusty #2), and Matt (the wisened agency client).

This cast of characters has been causing mischief and solving business problems in a non-identified city (that seems an awful lot like Atlanta, but I swear it's not) for years now, and it seemed like it was time to name this world. If for no other reason than it will be easier for me to refer to as I continue to write books in this series.*

Thus, I'm now going to refer to this world as the Turnaround Literary Universe (or the TLU for those of you "in the know.")

A bit silly to create a "name" for this business world I've created? Perhaps.

---

* *Oh, you bet I have ideas for more books in this series! There's* The Nonprofit Turnaround, The Life Turnaround, Always Lead with Purpose, *and* The Ninja and the Barbarian *(not technically in this series, but a children's book about finding a way to work together even though you're very different . . . but I digress), to name a few.*

Bold to mimic the greatest movie universe ever created and risk a potential lawsuit? Absolutely.

Am I doing it anyway? You betcha.

The Timeline

It's important to note that you can read this book independently, without having so much as glanced at the other books in this series. In fact, I've tried to write all of these books to be read without the need to read the others. Of course, they all build on each other, each tackling an area of business that every leader could learn from, and together they'll help you understand how to beat Thanos.

Below is a breakdown of when each of the books in the TLU (it's growing on you) was published, versus when they occur from a time perspective in the universe.

Order of Publication	Order in Story's Timeline
The 5-Day Turnaround	*The Culture Turnaround*
The Crisis Turnaround	*The Crisis Turnaround*
The Great Team Turnaround	*The 5-Day Turnaround*
The Culture Turnaround	***The Purpose Playbook***
The Purpose Playbook	*The Great Team Turnaround*

To be honest, it's all a bit confusing even to me, and I wrote the damn things, so I imagine it's also a bit confusing to you. So, here's what you need to know. If this is your first TLU book, then read on and see if you like the way the narrative plays out and the lessons that come from it. Then, if you enjoyed it, I'd recommend one of two paths:

If you want just a bit more, then pick up a copy of *The Great Team Turnaround*, as it essentially is the follow-up to this book. Or, if you're thinking to yourself, "I gotta see how this whole thing started," then grab a copy of *The Culture Turnaround*, which sets the stage for the entire series.

Speaking of the series, you can buy it in its entirety (signed if you really want to geek out on it), at the publisher's website: ripples.media/shop.

ONE MORE THING BEFORE
WE GET STARTED

We worked hard to create the most comprehensive book we could in order to help teams (and leaders) achieve their full potential by focusing on A) building trust, B) creating their PVTV (Purpose, Vision, Tenets, & Values), and C) relentlessly and forever-ly executing on A and B.

The entire process, as you know by now, is *The Purpose Playbook*.

In order to help you on your journey, we included a narrative so that you could picture yourself and your team going through this process, plus activities to help tactically guide you. We pulled from our experiences in running this process with our own teams, from countless consulting assignments working with partners going through their own journey, to examples from others who, over the years, have developed their own version of the PVTV and *The Purpose Playbook* methodologies (which we LOVE -> Mix and match, we say!)

We expect that as you make your way through the book, you'll find yourself flipping back and forth frequently from the narrative to the activities section, and back again. Please do not feel like you need to read this from cover to cover; we did not write it with that intention, nor do we feel it's the best way to absorb the content fully.

We diligently worked on this manuscript for a year and a half, going through rounds of edits and updates, while also implementing *The Purpose Playbook* for various teams, all the while capturing notes on what was working well and what was not, which further informed our process.

We have tried our best to create the essence and tactics of implementing *The Purpose Playbook* in the book you now hold in your hands.

And yet.

In all the times we have implemented this process, it has never gone entirely according to plan. There are always unique attributes to teams and individuals that require the process to be altered a little bit here and tweaked a little bit there.

Case in point, in the second half of 2023, we were working with an organization, and, after a solid half-day of progress, we began to hit a snag. Any time a particular aspect of their business was mentioned, the temperature in the room seemed to drop 10 degrees. People were mostly unwilling to speak up on this issue, and when they did, eyes would roll, and mouths would frown.

It became so apparent to us that we couldn't move forward without somehow getting past the dysfunction that this issue was causing, that we paused the entire process and called out the elephant in the room. What we learned was that this team had gone through a significant amount of "work trauma" and had yet to move past it.

We addressed the team leader and suggested that it would not be prudent to continue with our process until they were able to move through that trauma. They didn't need to solve the issue, per se, but they did need to make enough peace with it to begin building trust again within the group. Otherwise, our work on Purpose, Vision, Tenets, & Values would likely be contentious and incomplete.

Ultimately, the team leader agreed to spend the next hour with the team exploring the issue and, in an incredibly eloquent way, was able to coax everyone into a respectful yet impactful conversation. By the end of it, the entire group decided that they were ready to continue *The Purpose Playbook* process, which we did (to great success, I might add).

We share this story to recognize that, while some of you are trained consultants, most of you are not. This process can be sticky and messy and require agility that we simply couldn't capture in a single book.

So, while we encourage you to take on this process internally if you believe you have the ability to do so, we also want you to know that we are here if you need us. You can start by visiting **AlwaysLeadWithPurpose.com** to see how we can work with your team.

Whatever process you take, we want to make sure you are supported and put in the best position to be successful. Our mission, to have more businesses that are a force for good in this world, depends on it :)

THE STORY

PRELUDE

I*'m never going to get everything done today.*

This was the first thing that popped into Shera's mind as she woke from yet another restless night's sleep. It was the same thought she'd had at the start of every day lately.

Should my heart be beating this fast? And this early in the morning? That can't be good.

Shera couldn't remember the last time she awoke peacefully to her alarm clock. Back when she was working in corporate America, she was unhappy, sure, but most nights, she slept like a log.

But now, with her startup growing so quickly and all the inherent problems that come with that kind of growth piling up, she often found herself overwhelmed with the number of decisions she needed to make on an hourly – no, minutely? – basis, struggling to find enough hours in the day for all the work that was needed, not to mention that the team seemed to be arguing more than ever. What was the latest argument over? Oh, right, the creative team was arguing over why the vending machine didn't have enough diet products. As if that was worth arguing over. And how was she going to . . .

Ok, maybe this is why my heart is racing so fast.

She took a deep breath and tried to silence her inner mind.

Maybe this time, she could get herself back to sleep. What did that article say that she read yesterday? Repeat the word, "sleep," over and over again, and eventually, your mind will relax, and you'll fall back asleep. OK, let's give it a try.

Sleep . . . sleep . . . sleep . . . this is ridiculous. And why do we need so much sleep? Maybe humans only need five or so hours of sleep a night. Maybe it's Big Sleep that's been trying to convince us that we should be getting around eight hours of sleep . . . but why would there be an organization perpetuating this lie? Probably to sell drugs to us. Isn't it just like a drug company to . . .

With a sigh, Shera gave up on the idea of going back to sleep. Now it was time to see what ungodly time it was.

Please don't be in the fours. Ideally, it's at least six o'clock. I could even deal with 5:30 a.m., but please don't be in the fours . . .

Eyes still closed, she gently reached around the bed with her hand to determine where Fletch was so she wouldn't crush him when she rolled over. She knew he was in there somewhere. As ever since she adopted him from the local pet shelter five years ago, he would make his way into her bed at some point in the night. She found him curled up near her feet, a bit perturbed to be jostled awake at such an early hour.

She gave him an apologizing pat, then turned over to the other side of the bed to check the alarm clock that sat on the bedside table. Slowly, she opened one eye halfway, knowing what she'd see but hoping for a different outcome.

FOUR FREAKING 14 AM.

Great.

—

Getting up early was never Shera's thing. She had successful friends and colleagues who loved getting up early, like her rising star at work, Megan, but she always preferred to stay up late. And, when possible, sleep in.

She sat up and thought about what in the world she should do, given the early hour. Grabbing her phone off its charger on the bedside table, she opened it and immediately began to scan her email. Given that she checked her email a mere five hours ago (a habit she knew was bad for a number of reasons, but had yet to be able to stop herself from doing), she wasn't surprised to see that, other than a few newsletters she subscribed to, there wasn't much new in her inbox.

The next thing she did was open up the Calendar app to see what was on her schedule. The day was filled from start to finish, as it always was, with various meetings and appointments. Recently, thanks to a suggestion from her marketing agency CEO, Will, every Sunday night she color-coded the most important calendar item each day. Will had suggested she use green (which made sense, the guy was SO optimistic it was almost annoying), but Shera preferred red as it brought her attention more quickly to the appointment.

Sure enough, there was a bright red calendar item at 4:00 p.m. titled, "EVK Pitch." EVK was a prospect Shera's team at SalesLive had been courting for over six months, hoping their 200+ salespeople would soon have seats on the SalesLive software platform. The win would go a long way to helping her team hit their quarterly budget.

"Well, Fletch," she said, rubbing his head, "unless you have a better idea, I guess I should just get ready and head into the office." Fletch, having the much better idea of Shera staying in bed for the day with him, but unable to convey the message, simply dug under the sheets to stay warm.

—

Forty-five minutes later, Shera pulled into the empty parking lot at SalesLive. She rehearsed her opening for the EVK pitch on the drive, a habit she formed ever since getting her license at age 17 (her parents had the audacity to force her to wait until she was 17 to get her license, which, she regrettably came to believe, was a sound decision, as almost all of her friends who started driving at 16 got in an accident). Her goal with any speech or presentation was to have the opening three to five minutes memorized by heart, giving her the ability to deliver it in a casual manner. Shera was an excellent presenter, and the art of "rehearsing until casual" was at the heart of why.

She wasn't used to getting to the office before everyone, and she took the opportunity to nab the parking spot closest to the front door. As she got out of the car, she looked up at the building they had recently moved into. It was everything she had wanted: located in a hip area of town, trendy architecture that had that "tech" feel to it, and lots of open space. She had been on a tour of the Google headquarters a year before and had taken copious notes on the things she liked (and the things she very much didn't like . . . they had "sleep pods" for crying out loud!), and she thought they had pretty much nailed their goal of making the office both approachable and ambitious.

Even though they had been in this office for a few months, she still got a tinge of excitement as she used her key card to enter the front door. The red light on the keypad turned green, the door clicked open, and she pushed herself inside.

Passing through the lobby, she made a mental note to figure out why it had been so hard to find someone to work the front desk. They didn't get many visitors, but when they did, she sure wanted someone there to greet them.

She made her way down the hall and into the massive open space where most of the team worked. They had designed the office to have as few individual offices as possible, instead opting to set up an environment where people were likely to bump into each other and share ideas. Someone she knew had called this "allowing for serendipitous interactions," and like any good entrepreneur, she knew when an idea was worth stealing.

Her standing desk was located against the wall at the far end of the room, facing out to allow her a view of the office. Her three leadership team members had desks near her – also out in the open – which allowed them to collaborate in real-time.

Over the years, her leadership team had changed both in team members and in structure, and she was now down to a three-person team: George, her Chief Operations Officer (COO); Vijay, her Chief Financial Officer (CFO); and Megan, her VP of Product. Megan was her longest-tenured employee and a bit of a Swiss Army knife type of leader, helping out where needed.

After quickly rechecking her email – nothing new – and reviewing her calendar for the week one more time, she began rehearsing her opening speech for the pitch meeting later that day, going over the major points she wanted to hit and thinking through what to emphasize By this time, she had it down pat, but another few rounds of prep never hurt.

Eventually, the office started populating with people. Rita arrived at 7:25 a.m., over two hours after Shera. She gave Shera a quick wave on the way to the breakroom, where a fresh pot of coffee that Shera had brewed was waiting for her.

By 8:15 a.m., the office was beginning to fill up, and by 9:00 a.m., it was in full swing. Many of the team members, once they greeted each other and filled their coffee mugs, would throw on a pair of headphones to block out the noise and get to work, something that Shera found was key to working in an open environment like this. It's amazing how listening to music or white noise with noise-canceling headphones in the middle of a large group of people can help you focus.

Shera had her headphones on and had yet to fire up her music playlist when she overheard a conversation across the room between two of her team members. The two women, both of whom were on the Account Services team, were commiserating about the weekend being over, with one of them commenting, "Mondays are the worst."

"Well, I guess that's why they call it 'work' after all," the other woman said.

Shera was a bit stunned. Was that really how people felt coming to the office each day? She remembered the passion everyone used to have in the early days, and there had been a new rush of excitement when they moved into this office a few months back . . . but had those feelings faded?

She opened up the leadership team meeting agenda for that morning on her laptop and added a bullet to discuss team morale, and, realizing she hadn't sent the agenda out to the team yet, she polished it up a bit and sent it off. She had really meant to send the agenda before the weekend, but they'd still have a little time to review it before the meeting.

Her small but mighty leadership team, as she liked to refer to them, had been less mighty in recent months. Shera could deal with the team missing a few deadlines or not hitting goals from time to time, but they'd been arguing quite a bit lately, and many of their disagreements seemed quite personal.

Looking down at her phone, Shera chose a playlist she'd created called, "Harder, Better, Faster, Stronger," and began cranking away at her email inbox.

—

At 10 a.m. sharp, everyone was seated in the large conference room in the back corner of the office. Shera was at the head of the table, with Megan and Vijay seated to her right and George to her left.

After some quick banter back and forth – how was your weekend, crazy how great the weather has been lately, that kind of stuff – they began going through the agenda.

"Obviously, today is a big day with the EVK pitch this afternoon," Shera said. Megan was the only member of the leadership team who would be in the pitch with Shera, while both George and Vijay had been helping behind the scenes ever since they made it to the pitch round of the process. "Vijay, do you have the ROI numbers in a good place?"

Vijay's main role in a new business pitch process was to approve and refine the profit side of the relationship with the customer. In a technology business like SalesLive, it was a critical part of the process. "Yes, I tweaked it a little this weekend, but overall, I feel great about the LTV numbers, especially if we believe we can keep them as a customer for at least 18 months," he said.

Lifetime Value, or LTV, was one of the key metrics in their industry. Typically, it would take between nine and 18 months to begin showing profit on a customer relationship. The "stickier" the relationship — meaning, how difficult it was for a customer to switch to a competitor — the better. One of SalesLive's great strengths was how sticky their offering was, mainly because a customer would take many months to load all of their sales information into their system, at which point they'd be relying on the data from SalesLive to run their sales organization: a difficult thing to unwind.

"Vijay, I was reviewing your changes earlier this morning," Megan said, looking at her laptop, "and it seems like you cut a big chunk of the in-person onboarding meetings . . . "

"That's right," Vijay said, "I saved us a significant amount of costs by changing those meetings to virtual ones. We can get the exact same information as we would by being in person, without the associated costs."

"Yes, that's true, but remember we agreed late last year that those meetings were critical because of the opportunity to bond with the customer in those early, sometimes tenuous, first few weeks." Megan said.

Vijay looked puzzled. "I don't remember that, no," he said, looking at Shera. With a smirk, he added, "Is that part of our NESOPs?"

Shera frowned. "NESOPs" was a term that had recently taken hold in their leadership team meetings, much to her chagrin. It stood for Non-Existent Standard Operating Procedures. Meaning, they didn't have any Standard Operating Procedures, or SOPs. Which was true, but she didn't like being reminded of that fact. Mainly because that term very much irked George, who, as head of Operations, was responsible for developing their company's SOPs.

George cleared his throat and replied, "I would have to check my notes to see, but it does sound familiar. Shera, have you set up a time for us to go over the SOPs that should be at the top of the list for me to tackle?"

Shera tried hard not to roll her eyes. George had a bad habit of shifting blame to others when he hadn't made progress on a task, and insinuating that it was Shera who was holding up this process was not a true representation of the facts.

Not wanting to confront George in front of everyone, Shera

swallowed her pride and said, "No, I still need to get that on the calendar. However, I do remember this discussion and also thought we had agreed to keep the onboarding meetings as in-person meetings for the reason that Megan shared. We decided that those meetings were worth the investment."

"Fine, I'll force them back to in-person, but it would be nice if we had these things written down so everyone was on the same page," Vijay said, clearly annoyed and unable to resist getting in the last word.

Shera waited a few seconds to see if George was going to speak up and commit to working on the SOPs, but when that failed to happen, she said, "Thank you, Vijay, and we'll work on making progress on the SOPs."

"OK, anything else on the EVK pitch? Megan, feel ready to wow them with how you'll manage the account?" Shera asked.

"Absolutely!" Megan said, with the kind of enthusiasm Shera loved her for. "I think the entire team is ready for this one. It's been a while since we had an opportunity this big, so we scheduled an extra round of practice over the weekend."

"Great, love to hear it. Next on the agenda, I wanted to see if there was an update on finding a new receptionist. George, what's the latest there?" Shera asked.

George skimmed through his emails and said, "It looks like we've interviewed . . . this can't be right, but it says we've talked to over 20 candidates so far, had 12 in-person interviews, and extended two offers, but they didn't accept."

"I'm surprised we're having such a hard time with this. It's extremely important that we find this person soon," Shera said.

"I'm actually not sure it's very surprising," Megan said, jumping in before Shera could move to the next topic. "George, how many people have been helping in the process? Given that the team was overwhelmed, I was involved in a handful of the virtual interviews. And I ask because there didn't seem to be much consistency of team members in the meetings with me."

George thought for a moment and said, "Honestly, probably over 15 people because of what you said; everyone has been pretty overwhelmed lately."

"I wonder if that's part of the problem," Megan said.

"How do you mean?" Shera asked.

"Well, several of the people we were interviewing asked us questions — about the culture, about our goals, things like that — and we gave very different answers in each of the meetings I was in."

"Really?" Shera said. "I feel like I'm always talking to the team about those things. But OK, I'll think about it and come back with a plan on how to address that." Before anyone else could comment, she continued, "Moving on, it's also extremely important that we finalize the budget for next year. We have to get ahead of that so we are in a good spot before the holidays hit. Vijay, what's the update there?"

"Yes, I'm working on the budget, but if I can say something . . . it

35

seems like everything is 'extremely important' these days," Vijay said, using air quotes around "extremely important." "The pitch this afternoon, the SOPs, the budget, and even finding the new receptionist. I feel like everything has some kind of . . . manic energy to it nowadays, but we don't know how we're going to get it all done, or, more importantly, why we're focused on all of these things with such urgency."

There was silence in the room, and Shera was about to respond when George chimed in. "Yeah, I've always been a believer that if everything is a top priority, then nothing is. And I can't tell which thing we're focused on is the most important."

"Or why," added Megan.

"What do you mean, 'why'?" Shera asked.

"Well," Megan said, softly, "at times, it feels like we're just running fast to prove that we can run fast. Like, why are we pushing the team so hard all the time?"

"Yes, exactly," said Vijay. "We're pushing, pushing, pushing, but nobody really understands why. I mean, we all get that if the company grows . . . no offense, Shera, but we all get that you and the investors make more money the bigger we are, but that doesn't seem like a good reason to be pushing as hard as we are."

Shera was stunned. It felt like the team was turning on her. How did they not know where they were headed?

"You guys, I don't know what you're struggling with. Just last week at the company meeting, I reemphasized the core areas we are focused on. I spent a lot of time working on those, and I thought we were all in agreement," Shera said, struggling to hide her frustration.

It took a moment, but eventually, Megan spoke up. "It's true, you did, but . . . well, it was a long list of things, and nothing was passed out afterward, so I'm not sure if anyone can even remember them . . . "

"And two months ago, you gave a similar speech, and it was a completely different list," Vijay said. "As a matter of fact, I even went back and compared both lists, and there were very few things that overlapped."

George jumped in. "I think that's what we're saying, Shera. It doesn't feel like there's a thoughtful plan going on with the business. It feels like we're kind of just, like Megan said, running to run. Know what I mean?"

Shera knew one thing: she wanted to run out of this meeting immediately. How dare they accuse her of not knowing where the company was headed?

On the bright side, this was the first time she'd seen them all on the same page about something in a while. Small victories, she supposed.

Shera took a deep breath, and, not really believing her words but needing to get out of the conversation, said, "OK, I hear you all, and I understand. I'll need time to think about it. Ironically, the last item on the agenda is to discuss team morale."

She then shared with them the conversation she overheard about how, "Mondays are the worst," and the overall feeling that the vibe in the office didn't feel quite the same as it used to.

"I think we probably all feel the same thing," Megan said. "We've obviously gone through a lot of growth over the last year, and I think some of the new people we've hired haven't exactly been great additions. Our overall hiring process seems like it allows in people whom we wouldn't have hired in the past."

"I'm surprised you think it's a hiring issue, Megan," George said. "I've been hearing a lot of people arguing that you're pushing them too hard on the product side of things, and there's overall confusion about how to get things done."

Megan replied, "I wasn't blaming you for the hiring problems, but I also don't think it's exactly fair to suggest I'm pushing people too hard. We're understaffed in technology right now, so everyone is having to stretch a bit. I told you all this would happen when we opted to hire two more finance people instead of another developer."

Now it was Vijay's turn to become defensive. "Listen, I'm the last person who wants us to hire anyone unnecessarily, but we needed the extra person in finance to manage our growing business. It just makes common sense."

"Oh, and it doesn't make common sense to add to our tech team?!" Megan said, now clearly agitated.

Before Vijay could respond, Shera jumped in. "OK, enough. We all have varying levels of responsibility to bear for things not going as well as we'd like right now. But blaming each other isn't going to help anything. I think it might be best for us to take a break and clear our minds a bit. As I said, I'll spend time thinking about all of this, and I'll circle back with a plan."

George and Vijay grabbed their things and left the conference room. As Megan took her laptop and began walking to the door, she turned and said, "You know, if you need help figuring out a plan, just let me know. I — well, all of us — are here to help. Don't feel like you need to figure this out on your own."

Shera looked up at her and smiled. "Thanks, I appreciate it. It's a lot, for sure. We're all running a million miles a minute, and I think I just need to figure out how to come up for air for a bit to see the bigger picture. I'll definitely let you know if you can help."

After Megan left, Shera took another deep breath in, exhaled slowly, and closed her eyes. She could feel a headache coming on, and she was extremely tired. *Getting no sleep* and *having everyone complaining about everything* will do that, she thought.

But the pitch was in a few hours, and she'd need to be on the top of her game for it. Time to rehearse a little more.

—

A few minutes before 4:00 p.m., Shera greeted the EVK clients at the front door. There were six of them: three men and three women. She led them back to the conference room, pointing out different aspects of the office that she thought they'd find interesting along the way.

Megan met them in the conference room, along with the lead creative on the pitch and three other team members. The room was set up with a drink and snack stand in the corner, notepads and pens on the table, and the large screen monitor in the front already keyed up with the following slide:

WELCOME EVK,
IT IS OUR GREAT DELIGHT TO HOST YOU TODAY FOR A
CONVERSATION
ABOUT YOUR BUSINESS.

Shera always liked to frame pitches as conversations, suggesting they'd be talking about the client's business rather than about her own company. The more she was able to get the customer talking about their company, their challenges, and their aspirations, the more she was able to tailor the offerings of SalesLive to meet their needs.

Everyone sat down and made small talk until Shera asked if they were ready to get started. The room quieted and Shera stood up, as was her custom when kicking off such a meeting.

In her mind, the opening to a sales pitch was both incredibly important and, at the same time, the most inconsequential part of the entire process. Everyone with any experience in business had been to a big, important meeting where some blowhard (her father's expression) would use the chance to wax poetically about God knows what, trying to make some giant gesture in order to win the business right then and there. Meanwhile, everyone in the meeting felt uncomfortable, waiting for the real meeting to actually start.

Or, as was the case in her last job, the leader essentially punted on the responsibility to open the meeting at all, simply greeting everyone, thanking them for coming, and getting on with the show.

Shera, instead, took the opportunity to do a few things. First, she wanted to set the tone for the rest of the meeting, namely ensuring that this would, in fact, be a conversation rather than a presentation, where everyone was encouraged to engage, challenge, and weigh in. Her style would be casual and, at the same time, focused, ensuring the customer that they'd enjoy working with her team from a relationship standpoint but could also expect results. Lastly, Shera knew that how she delivered her opening could help relax her team a bit, as everyone was at least a little nervous in a sales pitch. A well-timed joke here, an inside reference, and her team would ease into the meeting and settle into their roles.

Shera had rehearsed her opening *ad nauseam* leading up to this moment. She'd done this kind of thing hundreds of times. It was her time to shine, and she was prepared.

Which was why what happened next took her by complete surprise.

—

"I want to extend a sincere welcome to you and the team, Barbara," Shera said, talking directly to the Chief Sales and Marketing Officer of EVK. "We've worked hard to be as knowledgeable about your business as we can be, and we look forward to today's conversation – and yes, I want this to be a conversation more than anything else.

"In fact, I'm going to sit down, because what kind of conversation would this be if we were standing while you were sitting!" Shera liked to use this act as a way to reinforce the back-and-forth dialogue she and the team would hope to have with the customer.

Shera smiled, looked around the room, and . . . completely forgot what she was going to say next. She had rehearsed this, to the word, and thought back to what she just said, repeating the last words in her head – *if we were standing while you were sitting* – but the next words simply wouldn't come.

Not knowing what to do, she saw the glass of water in front of her and decided to take a drink to buy time for her mind to stop acting like such a . . . blowhard. What did that word even mean, anyway? She might be using it incorrectly, but her dad had used it pretty liberally to describe anyone that he had an issue with. She put the drink down and wondered how in the world her mind could be working through the definition of the word blowhard right now instead of focusing on the problem at hand, namely, **what in the heck was she supposed to say next?**

Gathering herself mentally and reminding herself that she was a pro, she decided to just start talking, having faith that her mind would catch up to her words.

"The team at SalesLive is excited to share with you our overarching plan for how to help you grow your business," she said, "and I think you'll find our . . . "

42

" . . . our . . .

" . . . drive to, uh, succeed for our customers, far exceeds our . . . "

She looked around the room and saw the wide-eyed stares from her team members and the curious looks from the customers staring back at her.

" . . . what I think I'm trying to say is that, well, you've built up such a great business, and so have we, and . . . "

"And that is why," Megan said, "Shera told us to pull out all the stops when it came to preparing for this meeting. As the Product Manager over the relationship, I'll be running point on your business, so how about I introduce you to the other members of the team."

Megan introduced one of the team members and stole a quick glance over at Shera. Shera mouthed, "Thank you," to her, and took another drink of water.

What in the world just happened? She thought. *Thank God for Megan, otherwise I might still be shoving words together trying to make a coherent sentence.*

Was she shaking? She was shaking. She had to get out of there.

Shera leaned over to Barbara and whispered, "I'll be right back." Then, she stood up as quietly as she could and left the conference room. She quickly walked to the restroom, checked to see if anyone else was in there, locked the door, and looked at herself in the mirror.

What in the world is the matter with you? she asked herself. She looked like the old Shera, but inside her heart was racing and she was breathing too fast . . . was she having a panic attack?

She turned away from the mirror and began taking deep breaths, telling herself that everything was ok. But everything wasn't ok. She'd just made a fool of herself in front of a potential new client, and, even worse, in front of her pitch team. She had to get back in there because the team was probably worrying about her, and the last thing she wanted was for them to be distracted by her problems.

Four minutes later, Shera re-entered the conference room. A few people smiled at her, but most were engaged in a meaningful dialogue about EVK's competitive set.

The meeting continued as they had planned, and Shera was impressed that her team had handled her fumbling of the opening so well. At least they were prepared. She tried to stay engaged in the meeting, even offering a few comments, but mostly she couldn't stop thinking:

What the heck just happened to me?

And, more importantly, what am I going to do about it?

CHAPTER 1
TRUSTING TEAM

"Come on, Fletch, let's get going."

Shera was looking down at her tiny dog snuggled in the blanket on the couch. Her gaze rose, and she looked out the window into the front yard. It was a beautiful morning; she could hear birds chirping, and rays of sunlight were streaming in through the blinds. A perfect morning to go on a walk.

Fletch, however, was not at all in the mood. As soon as Shera entered the room, holding the leash (a dead giveaway that a walk was imminent), he dug deeper under the blanket. She sat down and gently uncovered him, saying, "You know, we go through this every day. You're not fooling anyone. You love walks more than I do."

He looked at her and sighed – do dogs sigh?! – and, begrudgingly accepting the fact that this walk was happening, climbed down from the couch, nailed a perfect up-dog stretch, and made his way to the door.

Shera clipped on his leash, opened the door, and was immediately struck by how bright it was outside. She grabbed her sunglasses and earbuds off of the small table in the foyer and closed the door behind her as they made their way through the driveway to the sidewalk.

They lived in a sprawling neighborhood just outside the city, at the end of a cul-de-sac, a priority to Shera when she was looking at homes. "Oh, do you have a kid?" the Realtor asked when she shared this requirement. No, she didn't; she just liked the idea of a little privacy, and, should she ever want to resell the house, she knew cul-de-sac houses would go for more.

They took a left on the sidewalk, as that direction led to the small park in their neighborhood, which was Fletch's favorite spot to do his business. As they walked — passing a neighbor mowing his yard, and a minivan backing out of a driveway — she began to talk to Fletch, as was her habit on their walks. (She always put her earbuds in as a ruse to fool people into thinking she was talking to an actual human.)

"OK, so here's the thing," she said. "I have the meeting with Charles tomorrow . . . of course I told you about that; you were the one who suggested it! Anyway, so we're meeting tomorrow, and I'm not exactly sure what I'm going to tell him." She liked to pretend that the two of them were having a real conversation. And she *had* told him about the meeting, and in their *conversation*, he had, in fact, suggested it.

Fletch's tail was wagging, which she took as a good sign to continue talking, though it was probably also because they were getting closer to the park.

"Of course, I want to be honest with him, but it's just so embarrassing. He thinks I'm this amazing entrepreneur, and ever since he invested in my company in the beginning, I've absolutely crushed it, so I can see why he thinks that. Why did he invest in the first place . . . Maybe because Will introduced us, but he probably saw something in me. In fact, I'll never forget the first time we had coffee, when he . . . what? Oh, right, I'm rambling. Back to the point — sorry. So you're saying I should be honest and tell him how I've been feeling and what happened in the EVK pitch . . . "

The gate to the park was open, as it always was, between the hours of 7 a.m. and 8 p.m. (according to the sign). As they entered, Shera pulled Fletch closer to her when a man walked past with a large Doberman Pinscher. Fletch, likely feeling bold with Shera holding him back, gave a slight snarl at the much larger dog and proudly pranced forward into the park.

They wound their way to the separately fenced-in dog park, which luckily was uninhabited at the moment. Shera unleashed Fletch and sat on the bench, watching him sniff and do his business everywhere so that he could tell another dog he had been there. *Boy dogs are so weird*, she thought.

She knew her meeting with Charles, as uncomfortable as it was for her to admit a weakness, was likely just what she needed. Just then, her phone buzzed. It was a text from Charles.

Hey Shera, looking forward to catching up tomorrow. I know you're a runner, and I've been working up to a half-marathon; any chance you want to meet at the main entrance to FP and go for a run-and-talk?

Interesting. She'd never had a running business meeting. But why not? She could use the exercise, as she hasn't felt like running for the past week. She had always loved visiting FP (or Foothills Park).

Shera sent Charles a thumbs-up emoji and scanned the park for Fletch. Sure enough, he was splashing around in the little pool area toward the back. As much as he acted like he didn't want to go on these walks, she knew it was always his favorite part of the day.

—

As expected, Charles beat her to the park. He was stretching near the bike rack as Shera approached. She always thought of Charles as the wise old mentor, but in reality, he was an extremely fit, late-middle-aged man. He was probably around 60 years old — she really had no idea — but he was more active than anyone she knew.

"Hey, there," she said as she approached. "Don't go pulling a hammy on me before we even start!"

Charles looked up, laughed, and said, "You know, I have very few regrets in my life, but not stretching when I was a younger man is toward the top of the list. When you get to be my age, you have to be extra careful not to get injured, because if you do, you'll be out for a lot longer than it would have taken to stretch."

They hugged. Shera pointed at the yellow bike he was next to and asked, "Is that your bike?"

"Sure is. I've put a lot of miles on this one; almost time to retire it," he said, patting the seat.

"Looks like it's in great shape to me," Shera said. "OK, so where are we going to run? A few loops around the park?"

Charles gave her a mischievous smile. "I had a . . . different idea."

———

Thirty minutes later, Shera found herself nearly out of breath, struggling to keep up with her running companion. It turned out that Charles' "different idea" was to go on a very hilly trail run rather than the flat path around the park that Shera had been anticipating.

"I didn't even know this run existed," she said, trying to talk in short sentences to mask how much oxygen she was sucking in. "Must be new. Have you run this before?"

"I haven't, but I kept up with the progress as they got closer to opening it, which I believe was about two weeks ago. You know, I was on the planning committee to build Foothills Park," he said. "If it's all right with you, let's take a break in a minute. There's meant to be a small sitting area near a stream up ahead."

Shera almost replied by suggesting that, sure, if *he* needed a break, they could take one, but decided instead to conserve her energy, and simply grunted out a "Sounds good."

A few minutes later, they came across a small wooden bridge that went over a narrow, flowing stream. There were a few picnic tables, a firepit that looked like it had been used recently, and a bench on the edge of the stream.

"Take your pick," Charles said, extending his arm toward the various sitting options. Shera chose the bench, and they took a seat.

"OK, so, what's going on that I can help with?" Charles asked.

"Well . . . I'm not quite sure, honestly. Something seems off, and I can't put my finger on it."

"How about giving me some examples of what's been happening," he said. "Feel free to ramble, and I'll just listen."

Shera started by reminding Charles of the growth they'd had over the last year, and how much she'd had to scale the team accordingly. He was aware, of course. As she suspected, he might be the only investor who read her quarterly updates in detail, but he asked a few pointed questions here and there for clarity.

She then spent some time talking about her leadership team, explaining how she had purposefully kept it small because they were a tight unit, but lately, they seemed to be in one of two states of being: arguing over inconsequential issues, or fighting for her attention.

"Hm, tell me more about them wanting more of your attention," he said.

Shera thought for a moment, then said, "Well, like the other day. George and I were meeting for a few hours to go over the plans for our SOPs. And we were meeting at the whiteboard behind my desk, which as you know, while that area has a little privacy, it is still in an open area. Several times during our meeting, Vijay popped his head in to ask questions, which, honestly, were all questions he didn't need me to answer for him. And then, as soon as George and I were done meeting, I noticed a block of time the very next day for Vijay and me to meet."

"So you think he was jealous of George because he was spending time with you?" Charles asked.

"I do, yes. There are other examples, and even Megan has done that kind of thing a few times." Shera looked at Charles and asked, "I mean, that's normal, right?"

Charles smiled and said, "It is normal, yes. What's also normal is for a team to begin to lose trust in each other."

Shera, a bit shocked, said, "I'm really not sure that's the case, Charles. What does that have to do with trust?"

"Let me start by saying that I could absolutely be wrong about this – no one knows your people better than you – and I can only speak from my own personal experience," Charles said "But when I've experienced team members who fight for the boss's attention and seem to be arguing more about what you called 'inconsequential issues,' it's because they are beginning to lose trust in each other," He used air quotes around "inconsequential issues."

"What makes you think I'm off on thinking the issues weren't important?" Shera asked.

Charles said, "Let's step back a bit first. There are typically three reasons that trust is lost within an organization: When someone loses faith in another person's ability to deliver, when someone doesn't think a person is being honest, and when someone doesn't think that another person is putting the team's needs in front of their own.

"Now," he continued, "share with me one of the times when your leaders were fighting over something that didn't seem that important to you."

"Hm," Shera said, thinking about what Charles had just shared. "OK. In a recent leadership team meeting, there were definitely a few times when people were questioning why another leader had made a decision that seemed to only benefit their department. Megan specifically wasn't happy that the budget was used for Vijay to hire more people in his department, but not in hers. I guess I wrote that off as a minor disagreement, but perhaps it's part of a bigger problem."

"Exactly. I imagine that you and Vijay, as your CFO, made the call on that?" Charles asked. Shera nodded her head. "So, going back to the three reasons that trust typically breaks down," Charles went on, "I hardly doubt that Megan thought you two weren't being honest, and she must think you're competent enough to make that decision, so she likely didn't think Vijay was putting the overall team before his finance department when advocating for more people."

"That's more or less what she said, yes," Shera said. "And now that we're talking about it, I don't think a year ago she would have questioned that. Those two used to be very close, but lately, we've all been so busy that I doubt they've spent much time together."

"You know, our mutual friend, Will, has had to work hard to overcome what happened to him early in building his agency. He trusted in the wrong people, and it came back to bite him," he said.

To learn about what happened to Will and his team, read *The Culture Turnaround*.

"Oh, I'm aware of that. It was before we started working together, but he was willing to share the story with me as I had heard rumors," Shera said. "So what has he done since to help him build trust with his team?"

"Well, he started by having me run a Trust-Building Workshop with his leadership team. After that, it's an ongoing process to keep moving to a place of trust, including spending more time together, which you already pointed out that your leaders haven't been able to prioritize lately. As they say, trust is hard to earn and easy to lose."

He stood up. "Let's start heading back down before that rain cloud gets to us."

Shera knew how valuable Charles' time was and couldn't decide if she should ask him to run the workshop with her team. When they were about halfway down the trail, she worked up the courage and said, "Uh, so, here's the thing, Charles. I was just wondering if . . . "

Before she could finish, Charles said, "Of course, I'd be happy to. What took you so long to ask?"

—

It took two weeks to align everyone's schedules for the full-day workshop that Charles agreed to run. Charles had made it clear that they should do this offsite, in case things "get intense," so Shera booked a room at a hotel she liked in town that had a great conference space overlooking Foothills Park.

She met Charles in the lobby at 8 a.m., and they took the elevator up to the seventh floor. The rest of the team would be arriving by 9 a.m.

They entered the conference room, and, as agreed by the building, there was coffee, water, tea, and sodas set up in the corner, with basic pastries and snack bars for breakfast. In front of each chair at the conference table was a pad of paper and a pen, and in the middle of the table, there was a basket of candy and snacks, which Shera made sure to have in long meetings. Sometimes a handful of Skittles was just what the doctor ordered.

Charles grabbed the seat at the head of the table and pulled out his laptop. He said he wanted to get there early in order to set up and prepare, so Shera decided to let him do his thing. She felt a sense of relief that she wouldn't have to run the meeting, giving her a chance to participate completely in the process.

She had told the team the main reason for the meeting — to talk through any issues they might be having as a leadership team — and asked them to clear their schedules, plus come to the meeting with open hearts and minds. If there was any confusion on their part, they didn't show it. It was as clear an indication as she could ask for that they also felt like their team wasn't in sync the way they used to be.

At 8:30 a.m., Charles looked up from his laptop. "So, Shera," he said. "How are you feeling about today?"

"I'm excited," she said. Seeing that Charles wasn't quite buying that, she added, "No, really. I mean, look, I don't know exactly what we're about to go through, and I'm a bit curious that you said the meeting might get intense, but overall I know this is what we need."

"And what is it that you think the team needs?"

"To get on the same page and to begin trusting each other again," she said.

"Great, that's exactly what I hope today's process will kick off. I do want to say, though, that I think this is just the first step in several that you'll likely need to go through. There are things that I think you're missing in the organization that, while always important, are even more important now that you've experienced so much growth. But before you can tackle any of those areas, you first have to start with a trusting leadership team."

Before Shera could respond, she heard a knock on the door. Megan poked her head in and said, "Hi! I know I'm early, so I can come back in a little bit if you two need to . . . "

"Come on in," Shera said, opening the door and giving her a hug. "Why am I not surprised that you're early? And you remember Charles."

Megan and Charles shook hands, then Megan put her stuff down at a chair and went to grab a cup of coffee. Over the next 15 minutes, Vijay and George also arrived, and everyone seemed to be in good spirits though also a bit cautious. It reminded Shera of a word that she and her mother used when she was growing up: "Nervcited." A combination of "nervous" and "excited."

At 9 a.m. on the dot, Charles stood up and said, "Ok, is everyone ready to get started?"

Heads nodded around the table, so Charles continued.

"I want to thank you all for coming today, as I know you have busy schedules. Hopefully, coming out of our session, you'll feel like the time is worth it. In order to ensure that can happen, I want to share some ground rules for our time together."

He walked over to the rolling, double-sided whiteboard that Shera had seen him writing on earlier. It simply said, "Welcome," on the side they could see, and he swung it around to show the back. It read:

TODAY'S GROUND RULES

BE PRESENT, NO MULTITASKING
(there will be time for breaks)

SPEAK UP

BE HONEST AND OPEN, YET RESPECTFUL

TRY NOT TO BE DEFENSIVE

REMEMBER THE GOAL

Charles sat down while everyone read the board. After a few moments, he said, "So, do all of these make sense?"

Vijay spoke up first. "I think the only one I'm not sure about is, 'remember the goal.' I'm not sure we've been told the goal for today's meeting."

Charles smiled. "Perfect. That is absolutely the right question, Vijay, and thanks for speaking up and asking it. I asked Shera to be intentionally vague about what we were doing today, for several reasons. I wanted you all to come into the meeting without any preconceived notions as to what we'd be doing, and to be open to new ideas from your teammates. Understanding the goal of today's meeting will be the first thing we discuss. Before we do, let me quickly run through why the other ground rules are important.

"It's critical that we are all present during this meeting, and I'd add that you should be present in ALL of your meetings together . . . and actually, in all meetings you have with anyone, period. Back in my day, we didn't have any alternative to being present in meetings, but today with laptops and phones, it's hard not to be distracted. So we're going to go through today's meeting with no electronic devices at all." Charles then closed his laptop, showing them that he was as equally committed to this process as he wanted them to be.

"Each of you is here because you're an important part of this company, and so it's very important that you speak up. We'll be talking about 'trust' a lot today, and a trusting team is one that feels free to speak up and share their opinions. This is something you'll work on going forward, but especially today, everyone needs to be heard.

"And when you are speaking up," he elaborated, "make sure that you're honest, open, and also respectful. I'm going to ask you to be more honest in today's meeting than perhaps you ever have been in your business career."

Shera, strategically positioned at the back end of the table, scanned the room to see how the group was taking the ground rules so far. Megan seemed to be in the same state of "nervcited," while Vijay looked a bit concerned. She couldn't tell what George was thinking, but he looked to be in good spirits. She was confident that *she* could handle this, but she hoped her team would be able to step up.

Which was why she was surprised to hear Charles call her out directly. "Shera, this will likely be hardest for you: being honest and open with the team, but also not being defensive," he said.

Astutely reading the look of shock on Shera's face, he quickly continued. "Don't worry, I'm not saying this because I think you're a dishonest person or that you get more defensive than others. Quite the contrary. You know I hold you in the highest regard. But . . . you care about this company, and in particular, this team, more than anyone. I'm going to be asking you to share things with them that will be uncomfortable, and I know you only want to support them and lift them up. But today is about breaking down walls and making progress toward building trust."

"I get that. I do love you guys," Shera said, looking at her three leadership team members. "OK, Charles, I'll try my best to be open with my feedback. But why are you worried that I'll be defensive? I can take the team sharing things that I need to work on."

"Oh, I have no doubt about that. I just want you to be ready to hear feedback about *your company*. Sometimes it's hard to hear that our baby isn't as perfect as we think it is," he said. "And as well as things have gone over the last few years, I think you're going to find that there is a lot of work to be done to get things on the right course."

Ouch. The first bit of defensiveness started to rise up in Shera, but, remembering the advice Charles had just given her, she swallowed it down and simply gave him a polite nod.

"And so," Charles said, "that leads us to the big question: what is our goal today? I'm sure you are all familiar with Patrick Lencioni. He wrote many of my favorite business books, and in fact, I learned much of what we will do today from his book, *The Five Dysfunctions of a Team*. He has a great quote from that book that I want to share: 'If you could get all the people in an organization rowing in the same direction, you could dominate any industry, in any market, against any competition, at any time.' Do you agree with that?"

Everyone nodded, but no one said anything, so Charles went on: "Come on, guys, this is the time to start speaking up. Do you believe that if you could get everyone at SalesLive rowing in the same direction, you'd dominate the industry?"

"Sure, it makes sense," George said. "But . . . well, if I was playing Devil's advocate, I might say that a team could be rowing in the wrong direction, right? So even if they're all rowing in the same direction, if they're off course, then they wouldn't dominate anything."

"Excellent point, George," Charles said. "And that is exactly the problem I've had with this quote. Lencioni's mostly focused, in this book, on building trust within a team, but if that team isn't headed in the right direction, what does it matter? This is why I believe this process we're about to go through is only the first step in your path forward. But we'll get to that later."

He wrote the quote on the whiteboard, only he crossed out "same" and wrote "right":

> *If you could get all the people in an*
> *organization rowing in the ~~same~~ right direction,*
> *you could dominate any industry, in any market,*
> *against any competition at any time.*

"How does that look?" Charles asked.

Again heads nodded, and this time Shera spoke up.

"I like it because it implies that they're all rowing in the same direction, but also stipulates that it's the correct direction."

"Exactly," Megan added. "And wouldn't it be nice to have that in the company right now? I feel like in the early years we had that – a direction we believed in that we were all focused on – but now . . . not so much."

Charles sat back down and said, "OK, so now that we agree on that point, I assume we also agree that in order to do that, this leadership team must be rowing in the same direction and that currently, you are not."

He looked around the room at each of them. They seemed to want to agree but were hesitating to say it.

"Guys," Shera said, "it's OK. I know we aren't on the same page; that's why we're here. You don't have to worry about hurting my feelings. I've raised my hand for help, and Charles is here to get us back on track. Right, Charles?"

"Right," he said, glad that she had broken the ice on that issue. "So, with that in mind, let's start seeing where you all want to take the company."

He stood up and walked over to the whiteboard. He wrote:

WHAT DO WE HOPE THIS COMPANY WILL BECOME?

"Now we're going to talk about your hopes and dreams for this company. Rather than shouting out ideas, I'd like everyone to take ten minutes to write ideas on the Post-it notes on the table. One idea per Post-it. That way, you aren't influenced by your team members," he said.

For the next ten minutes, the team filled up a few dozen Post-its. George struggled to get to five, while Megan wrote close to 15. Eventually, Charles went around and collected them all.

He then began sticking the Post-its on the wall behind Megan, organizing the ones that were similar. Once he was done, he looked at each of the grouped Post-its, combined a few more, and put the one on top of the others that captured the spirit of the group. He then wrote the final groups on the whiteboard:

KNOWN AS BEST IN INDUSTRY
LONG-TERM TEAM MEMBERS
HIGHEST CALIBER TECHNOLOGY
HEALTHY FINANCES

"How do these look to you? Did I capture everything that you wrote?"

They looked at the board, and Megan said, "I had one about having the best culture, and I see you put that under the 'Long-Term Team Members' group. I'm just wondering if that should be flipped, as it seems like having a great culture is really important."

She was looking at Charles for an answer, but he gestured to the rest of the team to respond. Finally, George said, "I could see that, though we also had one about being an attractive place to work, and then another about having amazing benefits, and Charles grouped them all under 'Long-Term Team Members' . . . who wrote that one, anyway?"

"I did," Vijay said. "And that was honestly the spirit of what I wrote. I was thinking about several of those things you just mentioned – great benefits, amazing culture – and I kept coming back to the idea that if we have long-term team members, especially in our industry, then we must have all of those other things, plus more."

Everyone seemed to agree with his logic, so Charles decided to move on.

"Anything else need to be changed with these? They aren't set in stone – yet – but they're at least a good starting place for the rest of our conversation today."

Charles looked at his watch and said, "OK, we've been going for about 90 minutes. Let's take a 15-minute break so you can check email, and then we'll get back to it."

During the break, Shera took a few minutes to check her email. She responded to a few, but after a couple of minutes, she closed her laptop and looked up at the whiteboard. Those things listed were very ambitious and in complete alignment with what she very much wanted for the company. Was this the leadership team that could get them there? Or, for that matter, was *she* the leader they needed?

Several minutes later, Charles re-entered the room and sat in his seat. He flipped through a few pieces of paper he had brought, made a note on one of them, and looked at his watch.

"OK, team, let's get back into it," he said. Shera couldn't help but smile as all of her team members were already in their seats by the time Charles had even come back into the room. They were, if nothing else, an on-time team.

Charles stood up and walked over to the whiteboard. He drew a line down the middle of the whiteboard, with the *"HOPES"* list on the left, and on the right side wrote: *"COMPETITIVE ADVANTAGE."*

"Now, we're going to have a bit of a debate. I'm curious what you all think our competitive advantage is, or should be, to allow us to achieve this," he said, pointing at the "HOPES" list.

"Who has a suggestion as to what our competitive advantage would need to be?" he asked.

This time, Vijay spoke up first. "Well, even though it's on our 'HOPES' list, I think our technology should be our competitive advantage."

Charles wrote that on the board, and turned back to the group. "Great, we'll debate these in a moment. Who else has a suggestion?"

"The relationships with our customers?" Megan said, more as a question than a statement.

"Tell me more about that," Charles said.

"Well, I feel like if we have extremely close relationships with our customers, and we're incredibly diligent about keeping and growing those relationships, that could be something we do better than everyone else," she said.

Charles nodded and wrote "Customer Relationships" on the board.

"Our process!" George said, almost shouting. "I mean, ultimately, we would need to create this, but if we had a great process that we followed when building our products, that could be our special sauce."

Charles wrote that on the board, then turned and asked, "What else?"

Shera said, "What about our culture?"

"Ooohh, I like that," Megan said.

Charles nodded, wrote that on the board, then asked for any other ideas. Ultimately, the group suggested a few more, with the final list being:

COMPETITIVE ADVANTAGE:

OUR TECHNOLOGY
CUSTOMER RELATIONSHIPS
OUR PROCESS
OUR CULTURE
SIZE / SCALE
LOCATION

"A true competitive advantage is one that is near impossible for a competitor to copy. When you look at this list, which of these would be extremely difficult for our competitors to replicate?" Charles asked.

No one said anything for a few minutes as they pondered this question, so Charles said, "Let's come at this from a different direction. Which of these would be easy for our competitors to replicate?"

"Location is an easy one. Heck, there are a few competitors in our city today," George said. Charles crossed off "Location."

"Size is also something that can be replicated pretty easily through acquisitions," Shera said. "And any competitor could get ahold of our process documents and begin to replicate them pretty quickly."

"Both true," Charles said, crossing them both off.

"I know it would be tough, but companies have found ways to copy each other's technology before, so I don't see why that couldn't happen to us," Vijay added.

Charles crossed off "Technology," and turned back to the group.

"I know I added this one, but I'm not even sure 'Customer Relationships' could be a competitive advantage. I mean, we can be very good at that, but is it really a differentiator?"

Charles let the group discuss that for a few moments, coming to the conclusion he knew to be true: customer relationships, while incredibly important, were not a competitive advantage.

"That just leaves us with 'Our Culture.' And while I think a company's culture can be unique and compelling, I'm not sure it can be a real differentiator. Your culture impacts your product, sure, but not directly. It impacts your financial health, but not directly. I'm not trying to downplay the importance of culture, not by any stretch, but as far as competitive advantages go, it's a hard one to really buy into."

He crossed off "Our Culture," and then added, "But there is something else that I think you all missed that directly impacts everything you have on this list, and that I believe is the key to unlocking all the items you have on your list of 'Hopes.'

"What would it take," he asked, "to accomplish having great technology, great customer relationships, great processes, a great culture . . . basically, to be great?"

Megan said, "Great people, right?"

"Aha, now we're getting somewhere," Charles said. "But, what does it require to have great people?"

They thought for a minute, and then it hit Shera.

"A great leadership team!" She shouted, startling everyone in the room. "Sorry, I got a little excited there. But that's the answer, isn't it? Without a great leadership team, you can't accomplish any of those things. You can't have a great team of people if the leadership team isn't stellar."

Charles said, "And a great, or stellar, leadership team is one that is united and trusts each other."

Charles walked up to the whiteboard and wrote:

OUR GOAL: TO BECOME A UNIFIED, TRUSTING LEADERSHIP TEAM

"What I want to sink in with all of you is that, if you can come together as a leadership team and build real trust in each other, and if you're all on the same page as to where this company is headed, then you can accomplish literally *anything*. Including this list," Charles, once again pointed at the "Hopes" list.

"Before we start that process, however, I want to see where we are today. You all have Post-it notes in front of you. I want you to think for a few minutes about this team. I know you all care about each other, but I want you to think about how well you think this team is actually performing as a unit.

"Now, on a scale of one to five, I want you to grade how you think the team is performing. A grade of one means the team couldn't be performing worse than it is now, and a grade of five means it couldn't be performing better. Don't worry; your answers will be anonymous, but I'm going to average them out and share the score with all of you. And then, at a future date, we'll reassess and see what kind of progress we've made."

Shera was struggling to figure out what her number would be, and thus was surprised when Megan quickly wrote her number down, folded her paper, and handed it to Charles. *I wonder what she wrote?* Shera thought as she stared at her blank Post-it.

On one hand, the team is made up of very strong members, each with an area of specialty that the company needs. On the other hand, they were arguing more than they had been, and it seemed like there was some jealousy happening between them . . .

George and Vijay both handed their folded Post-its to Charles, leaving Shera as the last to report. *I bet most of them graded us with a four. After all, I was the one who asked Charles to have this meeting, it's not like any of them had said there was a huge problem . . .*

She wrote a four on her page, then crossed it off and wrote a three, then immediately crossed that off and wrote a four again. Figuring there wasn't any more room on the Post-it to change her mind again, she folded it up and handed it to Charles.

Charles opened each Post-it, jotted down the numbers on his notepad, and averaged them together. He then got up and wrote:

CURRENT LEADERSHIP TEAM GRADE:
2.25

Shera was speechless. *Charles must have made a mistake,* she thought. *How could they receive an average of 2.25 if she alone gave them a four?*

"Does anyone have any questions before we move forward?" Charles asked.

Megan asked, "I'm curious. Is that a typical grade for a leadership team before they go through this process?"

"Oh, I've seen all ranges," Charles said, "but usually, if I'm meeting with a team, then there was most likely a bit of dysfunction that brought me there. I would say a grade between two and three is pretty common.

"But," he added, making sure to make eye contact with Shera, "I would say this team is in pretty good shape for receiving a 2.25 grade. There are many positive aspects to you as a group, including your obvious willingness to go through this process. So, there's a lot of good here, and I think we'll make great progress if everyone can keep the positive attitude you've already shown me."

That made Shera feel a little better . . . but only a *little*. How had she been so unaware of how her leadership team was feeling? A *2.25?!* She'd never received such a low grade in her life. *So this is what imposter syndrome feels like*, she thought.

Charles reached into his backpack and pulled out a folder. He took out a stack of paper and said, "Now comes the tough part. The only way we can begin building trust as a team is to give each other feedback about the behaviors that are leading to the dysfunction that we're experiencing.

"Starting with," he added, "a list of questions that you will answer about each other."

He passed out a sheet with the list of questions.

"You'll notice at the top it shows the range that you'll be using, with three representing a 'usually' answer and one representing 'rarely.' Read through the questions and tell me if everything makes sense," Charles said.

The team read through the questions, and asked a few clarifying questions, but otherwise, everyone felt like it was a fairly straightforward list.

Charles then gave everyone three scorecards, one for each of the other team members.

"On this scorecard, you'll write the name of the team member you're evaluating at the top, and then you'll notice that each question corresponds to a box. For instance, you'd write your answer for question one in the first box under, 'Theme One.' Does that make sense?"

Everyone nodded their heads.

"Great. Usually, it takes about ten minutes per person," Charles said, "so how about I give you thirty minutes to fill the sheet out for each of your teammates? Does that work for everyone?"

Heads nodded again, and Charles exited the room.

For no particular reason, Shera decided to start with George. She wanted to take her time and really think through each item on the list in terms of how it related to George. After George, she made her way to Vijay, diligently thinking about her CFO and how she felt about him in the context of the questions.

Last, but certainly not least in her mind, was Megan. By now, she knew the questions well and moved quickly through the assessment of Megan, smiling as she did.

After finishing the assessment of each of her team members, she then tallied them and began to compare how they scored versus one another. A few of the results surprised her.

Charles came back into the room, shut the door behind him, and said, "Is everyone done, or do you need a few more minutes?"

Seeing that everyone was done, he continued:, "Now, I'll need about 15 minutes to tabulate these results. But before I give you all a break, you have one more sheet to fill out."

Charles gave each of the leaders another page with the same questions and scorecard. "You're now going to evaluate yourselves, and when you're done, pass them to me."

Vijay said what everyone else was thinking: "Oh . . . great, we get to judge *ourselves* now. This should be fun."

Indeed, Shera had a very difficult time filling out the forms about herself. They all did. Eventually, they finished their self-assessment and handed their papers in to Charles, before taking a much-needed break.

Charles, sensing that the team was feeling a bit stressed and overwhelmed, decided to give them a little more time for a break. He was seasoned enough in processes like these to know that there are times you want to stick to a strict schedule, and other times you may need to change things up in order to get the best results.

"All right, everyone, time to get back into it," Charles said after ten more minutes had passed.

"What we're going to do now is, without a doubt, the most difficult part of our process. But it's also the most important, so I'm going to ask all of you to do your best to be honest and speak up, even if you think what you're saying will hurt the other person's feelings. We are here to get better and improve, and we can't do that without everyone participating in the process.

"When it's your turn to *receive* feedback," he went on, "I'm asking all of you to do so with grace. I'm not going to ask you to fight the urge to feel defensive – that would be impossible – but I am going to ask you to try not to react openly in a defensive manner. I want you to expect to hear difficult things and to receive that information in a constructive way. We want to use the feedback we hear today to grow and become stronger individuals, and, ultimately, a more trusting and cohesive team.

"We're now going to talk through five key themes," Charles said. He walked over to the whiteboard and wrote:

Fostering Trust
Healthy Conflict
Building Commitment
Cultivating Accountability
Collective Achievements

"As I mentioned earlier, this part is influenced by Patrick Lencioni's book, *The Five Dysfunctions of a Team*," he said. "Part of your homework coming out of today's session will be to read his book and discuss it as a group."

Dear reader, we hope that you will also read Mr. Lencioni's book as a supplement to this one.

"Lencioni's framework presents common dysfunctions that teams face. But the root is crucial for us to understand and address if we're going to build a stronger team. Let's start with the first theme: Fostering Trust," Charles said.

"Trust is the bedrock of any successful team. Without it, we spend our time protecting ourselves instead of collaborating effectively. Signs of a lack of trust include holding grudges, not seeking help, hiding mistakes, and avoiding spending time together. Building trust is about creating an environment where openness and vulnerability are embraced," he said.

Megan asked, "How can we actively build trust within our team?"

"Great question," Charles said. "It involves fostering open communication, acknowledging mistakes, and encouraging team members to share their thoughts and concerns without fear of judgment."

"The next theme is Healthy Conflict," Charles said. He noticed a confused look on George's face. "George, what do you think this one means?"

George thought for a minute and said, "Honestly, this one is a bit odd to me. Is it suggesting that we *want* to have conflict?!"

"Yes, I know it sounds contradictory to building better relationships with each other, but actually, healthy conflict is essential for innovation and growth. When we avoid conflict, we miss out on diverse perspectives and creative solutions. Signs of conflict avoidance include superficial agreements, talking behind each other's backs, and a lack of constructive disagreement during meetings. We need to foster an environment where differing opinions are valued, and conflicts are resolved through open communication."

George asked, "How do we differentiate between healthy conflict and destructive fighting?"

"Healthy conflict is focused on ideas, not personal attacks.

It's about challenging each other to improve, leading to better solutions. Destructive fighting involves personal attacks, politics, and negative emotions," Charles said.

"I get it," George said. "And it's funny because I remember learning something about that during the marriage counseling my wife and I went through as part of our pre-marital planning. I think the counselor said something like, 'If you aren't ever disagreeing, then you're not communicating, because we're all humans. But we need to be respectful and trusting when we do disagree.'"

Charles nodded, and said, "That's a great anecdote; I hope you don't mind if I borrow that for a future meeting. Now, let's move on to the next theme of Building Commitment. Teams with low commitment struggle to make decisions, often delaying actions or missing opportunities. This can also stem from a lack of healthy conflict, as team members may not feel heard. Indications of low commitment include not supporting team decisions, overanalyzing without taking action, and revisiting discussions without reaching conclusions. Building commitment involves making collective decisions and actively supporting and implementing them.

"This is an incredibly important one," Charles emphasized, "so I want to make sure you all understand what this means. Vijay, what does this one mean to you?"

"I guess it means that we won't always agree with each other, but as long as we all feel heard, then we need to agree with the final decision, and when we leave the room, we're all committed to making that decision work," Vijay answered.

"Exactly!" Charles said.

"But," Vijay said, "how can we ensure that everyone is committed to decisions made by the team?"

Charles smiled and said, "Another excellent question. I'm curious what the rest of you think?"

Megan chimed in. "I believe communication is pivotal here. We need to establish a clear understanding of each team member's role in executing the decision. When everyone knows how their contribution fits into the bigger picture, it fosters a sense of ownership and commitment. It's not just about making a decision; it's about each of us actively playing a role in its success."

Charles nodded appreciatively. "Well put, Megan. It's about translating decisions into actionable plans, and ensuring everyone knows their part in the process."

Shera added, "I also think it's about acknowledging and respecting different working styles. People may have diverse approaches to implementing decisions. Some might prefer a detailed plan, while others thrive in a more flexible environment. We should find a balance that accommodates various working preferences to ensure everyone can contribute effectively."

Charles smiled. "Great insight, Shera. Recognizing and appreciating diversity in work styles contributes to a more inclusive and collaborative environment. Now, how can we address concerns or reservations during the decision implementation phase? Megan, any thoughts on that?"

Megan considered for a moment before responding. "Perhaps we could establish regular check-ins or feedback sessions where team members can express how the decision is playing out," she said. "It provides an opportunity to address any challenges or adjustments needed, ensuring continuous improvement and keeping everyone committed to the team's goals."

Charles nodded in agreement. "Excellent suggestion, Megan. Open channels for feedback are essential to address issues promptly and adapt as needed."

Shera smiled. "I agree with Megan," she said. "Additionally, creating a positive atmosphere where constructive feedback is encouraged, and mistakes are viewed as opportunities for learning can help maintain commitment. We're all here to support each other's success."

Charles concluded, "Fantastic insights, both of you. Building commitment is an ongoing process that involves clear communication, understanding roles, accommodating diverse working styles, and fostering a culture of continuous improvement. It involves creating an environment where everyone feels heard during the decision-making process and actively participates in shaping those decisions. Any final thoughts or questions on this before we move on to the next theme?"

No one had anything to add, so Charles said, "The fourth theme is Cultivating Accountability. Accountability is crucial for high-performing teams. Forgoing it leads to suboptimal performance and missed goals. Signs of accountability avoidance include resenting different performance standards, relying solely on the team leader for feedback, and avoiding direct conversations about performance with colleagues. Cultivating accountability means setting clear expectations, encouraging open feedback, and holding each other responsible."

"How do we handle accountability without creating a blame culture?" Vijay asked.

Charles was ready to answer. "It's a critical concern. Accountability is about learning and improvement, not blaming. It involves open communication, constructive feedback, and a focus on collective success."

Megan interjected, "But how do we make sure people feel comfortable holding each other accountable without fearing backlash or damaging relationships?"

Charles considered the question. "Excellent point, Megan. Creating a culture of constructive accountability requires building trust within the team. When there's a foundation of trust, people are more likely to see feedback as an opportunity for growth rather than criticism. We should encourage open conversations, emphasizing that holding each other accountable is for the benefit of the team and our shared goals."

Shera added, "I think having clear expectations from the beginning can also help. When everyone understands their roles and responsibilities, it becomes easier to hold each other accountable. It's not about pointing fingers; it's about ensuring everyone contributes their best to the team's success."

Charles nodded. "Exactly, Shera. Clarity in roles and expectations sets the stage for accountability. It's also crucial to recognize and appreciate efforts. Positive reinforcement impresses the idea that accountability is not just about addressing mistakes but also celebrating achievements and progress."

Vijay offered a suggestion. "Maybe we could establish regular check-ins in which team members discuss their progress and any challenges they're facing. It creates a proactive approach to accountability, allowing us to address issues early on and learn from them."

Charles agreed. "Great idea, Vijay. Regular check-ins provide a structured platform for accountability discussions. It fosters a continuous improvement mindset within the team."

George, reflecting on the discussion, said, "I like the idea of making accountability a positive and collaborative effort. It's about helping each other succeed rather than pointing fingers when something goes wrong."

Charles smiled. "Exactly, George. Accountability is a team effort aimed at our collective success. By fostering an environment of trust, clear expectations, positive reinforcement, and proactive communication, we can create a culture where accountability becomes a natural part of our team dynamic.

"Now we get to the final theme," he went on, "Collective Achievements. We often ignore team objectives and give precedence to individual goals instead. This can hinder overall success. Signs include a focus on personal career advancement, a lack of collaboration, losing to competitors, and losing talented team members. Addressing this theme requires aligning individual goals with team and organizational objectives, fostering a sense of collective achievement."

"How can we align individual goals with team objectives effectively?" Shera asked.

Charles was ready to answer. "That's a crucial question. It involves creating a shared Vision, communicating organizational objectives clearly, and ensuring that individual goals contribute to the overall success of the team and organization."

George spoke up. "I think sometimes individual goals and team objectives might clash because not everyone understands how their work contributes to the bigger picture. How can we bridge that gap and help everyone see the connection?"

Charles said, "An excellent point, George. It's essential for everyone to see the bigger picture. Regular communication about the team's progress and how each person's contributions fit into the overarching goals is crucial. Transparency helps everyone understand the impact they're making and keeps them motivated toward shared objectives."

Megan added, "Maybe we could also establish a system where each team member sets individual goals that align with the team's objectives. That way, everyone is accountable for their contributions, and we're all working towards the same goals."

"Great suggestion, Megan," Charles said. "Individual goal-setting aligned with team objectives creates a sense of ownership and personal investment in the team's success. It also encourages self-motivation and accountability."

"I can see how this connects back to trust and communication," Vijay said. "When everyone understands the 'why' behind their tasks, and they see the impact on the team, it fosters a collaborative mindset."

Charles smiled. "Absolutely, Vijay. Trust, communication, and shared understanding are interconnected. When we align individual goals with team objectives and communicate the shared Vision effectively, it not only enhances collaboration but also fosters a sense of collective achievement. Any other thoughts or questions on this final theme?"

George raised his hand next. "What about recognizing and celebrating individual and team achievements? How does that play into aligning goals?"

Charles replied, "Recognition is crucial for reinforcing positive behaviors and achievements. Celebrating both individual and team successes creates a culture where everyone feels valued and motivated to continue contributing to the team's objectives. It's an essential aspect of aligning individual and team goals for our collective achievement."

Feeling like the team was on the same page, Charles concluded by saying, "In understanding and addressing these themes, we can create a more cohesive and effective team. Let's work together to build trust, embrace healthy conflict, make committed decisions, foster accountability, and align our objectives for the success of our team and organization. Any more questions or thoughts before we move forward?"

"I have one," Shera said. "Which theme do you think is the most important?"

"I'm sure I should probably be more diplomatic so as to not hurt any of the other theme's feelings," Charles said with a wry smile, "but I think Fostering Trust is the most important. Of course, each of these themes build on each other and they're all needed to truly create a cohesive, trusting team, but it all starts with trusting each other.

"Which is a good segue," he went on, "into the next phase of this process, where we dive into each of your self- and team-assessments. And Shera, we're going to start with you. You rated yourself on the five themes, and the team also provided their ratings anonymously. Let's see how they align."

Shera, feeling a mix of confidence and apprehension, turned to face her teammates with a smile. "Sure, everyone. I think I'm in tune with the team, but let's see."

Charles scrutinized the scores. "For the first theme, Fostering Trust, you rated yourself a four, and the team rated you a four as well. Solid agreement there."

Shera, addressing the team, quipped, "Well, at least we all trust me as much as I trust myself. That's a relief!"

Laughter rippled through the room, breaking the tension. Even Charles couldn't help but chuckle. "Trust is crucial, and I want to make sure everyone feels comfortable within the team," Shera added, still grinning.

"Agreed. Now, for the second theme, Healthy Conflict, you gave yourself a three, and the team rated you a three, too," Charles continued.

Shera's confident facade wavered slightly. She thought she was sandbagging that one, hoping the team would rate her higher. "Fair enough. Conflict is healthy when it's constructive, but I know there's always room for improvement."

George interjected, "Shera, I think it's great that you're open to improving. We're all here to support each other."

Shera, appreciating the encouragement, smiled. "Thanks, George. I guess I need to sharpen my conflict-resolution abilities. Honestly, I don't love conflict so I do probably try to avoid it."

Vijay, known for his calm demeanor, chimed in. "Shera, I've seen you handle conflicts diplomatically. Maybe we just need more opportunities to engage in healthy debates as a team."

Megan, always the strategist, added, "Absolutely. Constructive conflict can lead to innovative solutions. Shera, maybe we could schedule more structured brainstorming sessions where we actively encourage diverse opinions."

Charles, pleased with the team's collaborative spirit, nodded. "Great suggestions, everyone. Shera, let's make conflict resolution a team superpower. Any other thoughts or questions on this before we move forward?"

Shera shook her head no so Charles moved on to Building

Commitment. "You rated yourself a four, and the team gave you a three. Any thoughts on that?"

Shera, now facing her team directly, responded, "I thought I was actively supporting our decisions. I'll make sure to communicate my commitment more clearly moving forward."

Charles said, "Team, when we talk about Building Commitment, we have to be mindful that we aren't hesitant to make decisions or reluctant to buy into the team's goals. It's not just about saying 'yes' in the moment but actively supporting and implementing those decisions once we leave this room."

He continued, "Commitment is about being all in. It's not just about agreeing during our discussions, but following through with actions that align with our collective decisions. It's about making those decisions as if they were your own, understanding that the success of the team is intertwined with your individual commitment."

George took a moment to share his thoughts. "You know, I struggle with this too. Sometimes I find myself hesitant to fully commit, thinking I might need more data or worried about whether it's the 'right' decision. It's not that I don't support the team, but I realize I need to work on showing my commitment more explicitly."

Shera appreciated George's honesty and vulnerability. "Thank you, George, for sharing. It takes courage to admit where we can improve. You're not alone in this journey. The important thing is that we recognize it and work collectively to strengthen our commitment. We got this!"

Megan chimed in. "Communication is key, Shera. Let us know how we can support you in making sure we're all on the same page."

Shera nodded appreciatively. "Thank you, Megan. And Charles, I understand now that it's not just about agreeing but actively showing that commitment. I'll make a conscious effort to ensure my actions align with our decisions."

Charles smiled. "That's the spirit, Shera. Building commitment involves continuous communication, understanding each other's perspectives, and ensuring our actions reflect our collective decisions. Any more thoughts or questions on this before we proceed?"

The team seemed to be ready to continue, so Charles said, "Cultivating Accountability. Shera, you scored yourself a three, and the team rated you a two."

Shera, genuinely surprised, turned to face her teammates. "A two? I thought I was holding myself accountable and encouraging others. Any specific feedback?"

Vijay, typically the most bold of the group, offered, "Shera, maybe we could use more direct feedback from you. It might help us all be on the same page."

Shera, with a mischievous grin, added, "And here I thought I was being subtle with my sneaky accountability suggestions!"

Everyone laughed once again, lightening the mood in the room.

Charles chuckled. "Subtle or not, direct feedback can be a game-changer.

Charles concluded, "Lastly, Collective Objectives. You rated yourself a four, and the team gave you a four as well. Good alignment there."

Shera, now fully engaged with her team, smiled. "Thank you all for the feedback. I want to ensure my goals align with the team's for our collective success."

Charles nodded, sensing the dynamics at play. "Overall, great self-awareness, Shera. It's fantastic that you're open to feedback. Anything you'd like to discuss further with the team?"

Shera, addressing her teammates, leaned in. "Thank you, everyone. I appreciate your insights. This process is crucial for our team's growth, and I'm genuinely committed to making positive changes. Your feedback means a lot, and I want us to continue being open and honest with each other."

The room held its collective breath, the drama unfolding within the team dynamics. Charles, orchestrating the conversation, nodded approvingly. "Excellent, Shera. That's the spirit. Now, let's move on to Megan's assessment."

Shera, however, took a moment to address her team further. "Before we move on, I just want to express how important this process is for all of us. Each piece of feedback helps us understand ourselves and each other better. It's not just about individual growth but about how we can become a stronger, more cohesive team. So, thank you all for your honesty."

Vijay chimed in. "Shera, it's great to see your dedication to the team's growth. I think this openness will foster a culture of continuous improvement."

Shera smiled appreciatively. "Absolutely, Vijay. Our team is our collective strength, and this process helps us unlock our full potential."

Charles, ever perceptive, added, "And remember, the goal here is not perfection but progress. Let's learn from each other and grow together."

As the team absorbed Shera's commitment and Charles' wise words, Shera added, "I'll be thinking about the feedback I received today, and I encourage each one of you to share your thoughts openly. Let's create an environment where we feel comfortable challenging each other and supporting one another. This is our journey together."

The atmosphere in the room shifted, with a sense of unity and shared Purpose settling in. The rest of the day progressed much the same, with the team evaluating each of their team members and healthy dialogue ensuing. Shera could tell that her willingness to be vulnerable had helped set the stage for the rest of the team to be receptive when hearing their feedback.

As the day wrapped up, Charles, with a thoughtful smile, looked around the room. "All right, team, excellent work today. Going through the Trust Workshop and these themes is a significant step for our team's growth. However, it's essential to remember that building trust is an ongoing effort. We've laid the foundation, but it's up to us to maintain it as we move forward.

"As we embark on this journey together," he continued, "keep in mind the importance of open communication, constructive conflict, commitment to decisions, mutual accountability, and alignment with our team objectives. These principles aren't checkboxes but guiding principles for our everyday interactions."

Charles leaned in a bit more, his tone warm and encouraging. "Building trust is like tending to a garden. It requires continuous care and attention. I encourage each of you to brainstorm ways we can actively cultivate and reinforce the trust we've started building today. It could be through regular check-ins, team-building activities, or even simple gestures that foster a sense of camaraderie. Let's commit to keeping these principles alive in our daily work."

He smiled at the team. "Congratulations, everyone. You've shown great insight, openness, and commitment today. Sleep well tonight, knowing that we've taken a significant step forward. Tomorrow is a new day for your team, and I'm excited to see how you continue to evolve."

As the team members began to gather their belongings and prepare to leave, Shera lingered for a moment, telling them she would clean up. When the room cleared, she took a deep breath

and reflected on the impactful day. *Today was a game-changer,* she thought to herself.

As she straightened chairs and organized materials, she couldn't help but feel a renewed energy within the team. The Trust Workshop had opened a door to a deeper level of understanding, and Shera was determined to keep that door wide open. The impact of the day lingered, setting the stage for a brighter future for their team.

—

Shera and Charles sat in a cozy coffee shop two weeks after the Trust Workshop, the aroma of freshly brewed coffee filling the air.

Shera smiled, stirring her coffee. "Charles, I have to say, the team has been making great progress since our Trust Workshop. We've implemented some of the strategies we brainstormed – more out-of-office experiences, and actively pushing each other for feedback. It's been transformative."

Charles nodded, pleased with the update. "That's fantastic to hear, Shera. Building trust is an ongoing journey, and I'm glad to see your team taking proactive steps. It's essential for a healthy, high-performing team."

Shera leaned forward, her expression thoughtful. "However, I've come to realize that for us to continue evolving, we need more clarity on the direction we're headed as a company. The changes we've made within the team are great, but we need a stronger foundation."

Charles smiled, recognizing the significance of this next step. "You're absolutely right, Shera. What you need to do, in my opinion, is create your Purpose, Vision, Tenets, & Values, or PVTV. Clarifying your PVTV is crucial for aligning the team and ensuring everyone is moving in the same direction. It's about defining your company's identity and creating a shared sense of Purpose."

Shera hesitated for a moment before asking, "I know I'm being greedy here, but is that something you can you help us with?"

Charles took a sip of his coffee and sighed, "I wish I could, Shera. However, I'm about to embark on a trip in South America, and I'll be away for a while."

Shera raised an eyebrow, a mix of surprise and curiosity. "That sounds incredible, what are you doing in South America?"

"We'll be spending a lot of time in Argentina and Patagonia, doing all sorts of activities. I think I'm most excited about hiking the glaciers."

"Woah, that does sound exciting," Shera said. "OK, so if you can't help us create our PVTV, who can?"

"Don't worry, Shera. I've got the perfect person in mind. Our mutual friend, and I believe your agency partner, Will. He's brilliant at guiding teams through the PVTV process. I've worked with him before, and he has a knack for bringing out the essence of what makes a team tick."

Shera's eyes lit up with interest. "Will? I love him!"

Charles chuckled, "Same. I promise you, Shera, he's the best person to help your team navigate this exciting journey."

As they finished their coffee and parted ways, Shera felt a renewed sense of enthusiasm. The journey of building trust within the team had set the stage for a more profound exploration of their company's identity. With Will's guidance, she felt they were ready to define their Purpose, Vision, Tenets, & Values.

It should be pretty obvious at this point that we are huge fans of Patrick Lencioni's books, in particular *The Five Dysfunctions of a Team*, which this section was inspired by. While we have our own spin on his process, you'd do well to have your team read his book to learn more about the process. If you would like someone to officially facilitate this process, Teresa is an Authorized Partner of The Five Behaviors®, a Wiley brand.

CHAPTER 2
PVTV

"The Steaming Cup, really?" Shera said to Will as they happened to both get to the coffee shop at the same time — five minutes before their scheduled appointment.

"What, too on the nose?" Will said as they exchanged a hug. He held the door open as she entered.

"No . . . well, yeah, now that you mention it. What I meant was that this seems to be where we always meet, unless it's at one of each other's offices. You're some kind of creature of habit, aren't you?"

"Guilty as charged. My mother always said I'd have had the same three friends, and done the same three things with them, if I hadn't been forced to join the tennis team back in the ninth grade," Will said.

They stood in the ordering line, and Shera said, "I thought maybe you'd want to meet up doing some kind of extreme sport or something. Seems like all my meetings with Charles involve exercise of some kind."

Will laughed and said, "Nope, not me. I leave those kind of meetings to the guy 15 years my senior."

They arrived at the front of the line and placed their orders; the guy working the counter asked Will if he wanted his "regular" (he did). Shera rolled her eyes and ordered a vanilla latte with almond milk.

"Ugh, you have a regular here?" she asked.

"Sure do, and it's easy to remember: black coffee with a splash of oat milk. Come on, let's sit in my 'regular' booth as well," he said, giving her a wry smile.

Sitting at the table, they made small talk for a few minutes and then Will asked, "So, Charles said you're on some kind of exciting entrepreneurial journey with your company. I've done a few of those myself, as you know. How can I help?"

Shera walked Will through the Trust Workshop and everything that led up to it, including, because Charles had pushed her to tell Will everything, the panic attack during the client pitch. She finished by saying, "And so, Charles told me the next step would be to create our PVT . . . "

"V," Will said.

"Right, PVTV, and that you'd be the best person to help me figure that out."

Will thought for a moment and said, "How long ago was the Trust Workshop?"

"Six months," Shera said. "Charles said we needed to make a lot more progress before I met with you."

"And you feel like you're 'there' at this point?" Will asked.

"I do, yep. It's amazing how much progress we've made as a team," she said.

"Tell me what you mean by that, and what you've done since the Trust Workshop to build the momentum," Will asked.

The late afternoon sunlight filtered through the café's large windows. The hum of quiet conversations and the occasional hiss of the espresso machine provided a comfortable backdrop.

Shera leaned back, her eyes reflecting a mix of pride and relief. "Will, it's like night and day. You wouldn't believe the change. There's this openness now, a willingness to share ideas and challenges without fear of judgment. It's like we've broken down these invisible barriers."

Will nodded, encouraging her to continue.

Shera took a sip of her coffee, choosing her words. "Take Megan and Vijay, for instance. They used to work in silos, but now there's this synergy between them. Megan's creative solutions are being realistically assessed and budgeted by Vijay, and they're actually enjoying their collaboration."

Will's eyebrows rose in pleasant surprise. "That's quite a shift."

"It is," Shera agreed. "And George, he's become more approachable. His team feels empowered to bring up issues directly, leading to quicker, more effective problem-solving."

Will smiled. "Sounds like you've built a solid foundation of trust."

Shera's expression turned contemplative. "Exactly. And that's why I think we're ready for the next step – building out our PVTV. The trust we've developed is the perfect foundation for this."

Will leaned forward, intrigued. "That's a big step. How do you plan to approach it?"

"We'll do it collaboratively," Shera replied with determination. "Each person brings a unique perspective, and I want all voices to be heard. This is about who we are and where we're going as a team, as a company. I want the PVTV to be a true reflection of us, not just a set of ideals on paper."

Will nodded, impressed. "Sounds like you're not just building a strategy, but a culture."

Shera smiled, a glint of excitement in her eyes. "Yes, we are. And with this foundation of trust, I'm confident we'll create something truly representative of SalesLive's essence and direction."

Will's interest was piqued. "You've made remarkable progress, Shera. But trust is an ongoing journey. What specific steps are you taking to continue building this trust?"

Shera set down her coffee cup, her expression turning reflective. "That's a key point, Will. It's about maintaining and nurturing the trust we've built. For starters, I'm encouraging more in-person interactions outside the office. Coffee catch-ups, lunches, even walking meetings. It's about breaking the monotony and formality of the office environment."

Will nodded approvingly. "A more personal touch. What else?"

"We're restructuring our meetings," Shera continued. "They're more interactive now, with a focus on engaging everyone. I'm pushing the team to delve into the more challenging discussions, the kind that require us to really listen and understand each other's perspectives."

"That can be tough," Will interjected.

"Yes, but it's necessary for deeper understanding and cohesion," Shera affirmed. "And on a personal front, I'm continuing to show vulnerability. Sharing my own challenges, doubts, and learning moments. It sets a tone, showing that it's okay not to have all the answers."

Will's expression showed his admiration. "That's powerful, Shera. Vulnerability is often the bridge to deeper connections. Anything else?"

Shera's eyes sparkled with enthusiasm. "Plenty. We're also integrating team-building activities that are not just fun but thought-provoking. And I'm encouraging mentorship within the team. It fosters a culture of support and growth."

Will leaned back, impressed. "You're really dedicated to this, Shera. It's impressive how you're embedding trust into the very fabric of SalesLive's culture."

Shera smiled. "It's the only way to ensure we continue to grow not just in size, but in strength and unity. As Charles explained, trust isn't just a goal. It's the path to everything we aspire to be at SalesLive."

As they finished their coffees, the conversation drifted to other topics, but the theme remained constant: building a culture of trust at SalesLive, a testament to Shera's leadership and Vision for her team's future.

—

One week later, Shera found herself at Will's agency, with Will introducing her to his company.

"For those of you that don't know her," Will said, "I'm excited to introduce you to Shera, the CEO of SalesLive. Shera is going to observe our monthly meeting. So let's not hold back, consider her part of the team!"

Everyone clapped for Shera, which made her feel a bit embarrassed, but she was glad to be welcomed so openly. She took a seat in the back of the room as the meeting started.

Looking around, she guessed that there were about 40 people in the meeting, and just the kind of diverse group you'd expect from a creative agency: a mix of well-dressed and properly groomed individuals (likely account service reps, she thought) and a large group of T-shirt-and-shorts-types, which she assumed were the creative part of the team.

Will said, "OK, as always, we'll start by having someone recite our PVTV. Who wants to go this time?"

After a few moments, a hand went up toward the left side of the room. Shera didn't recognize the person – she probably knew about a handful of the team members from their work together – but thought she was brave for stepping up in front of everyone.

"Sarah, great, thanks for volunteering!" Will said. "And I think this is the first time one of our interns has attempted our PVTV!"

Sarah smiled shyly and, nodding over to Rachel, said, "Well, Rachel said in our orientation that we should look for ways to stand out, so here goes, I guess . . . Our Purpose is to inspire happiness through positive relationships, impactful work, and doing good."

Continuing, she added, "Our Vision is to be sought after by the world's best companies for our creative problem-solving."

Sarah then explained how the company plans to achieve its Vision, mentioning attracting and retaining exceptional people, building remarkable products and services, and always trying to be better in what they do. "We believe in putting the team first, thinking positively, celebrating diversity, doing good, and having fun," she added, summarizing the company's Values.

Ending her speech, she said, "As I've heard you say, Will, we are building a forever company." As she finished, the room filled with applause. Sarah sat down, beaming.

Shera, observing from the side, felt a surge of pride. Sarah's words not only seemed to capture the company's essence but also reminded everyone of the shared commitment that united them.

"Before we move on," Will's eyes scanned the room until they landed on Shera, who was observing quietly from the side. "I think this is a perfect opportunity for us to share with Shera why we start each meeting by reciting our PVTV."

He looked around, encouraging his team members to speak up. "Anyone want to share their thoughts?"

A hand went up, and then another, as team members began to articulate their reasons. One mentioned, "It reminds us of what we're all working towards, not just our daily tasks but . . . the bigger picture."

Another added, "It keeps our Purpose front and center, making sure we don't lose sight of who we are as a company and how we want to impact the world."

"It's about unity," a third team member said. "Reciting the PVTV together strengthens our sense of community. It's like a team huddle before a game."

Will nodded, listening intently to each response. "Exactly," he agreed after the last team member had spoken. "It's our compass, guiding us in our decisions and actions. It ensures that every one of us, from interns to senior leadership, is aligned and moving in the same direction."

Turning to Shera, Will concluded, "It's more than just words for us. It's a commitment. It's what makes us, us."

Shera nodded back at Will. It was becoming clear to her why Charles had suggested her team needed their own PVTV. It was not just a ritual but the heartbeat of the company, a constant reminder of their collective Vision and the Values that drove them forward.

The meeting progressed from that point, with several leadership team members getting up to give updates on various projects and results. Shera thought the meeting flowed really well, making a few notes in her notebook.

As the meeting neared its conclusion, Will transitioned to the acknowledgements section. He began, setting the tone with sincerity and warmth. "Before we wrap up, let's move to a part of our meeting that's always been close to my heart — acknowledgements. As many of you know, this practice was inspired by something I saw in my kid's school, of all places, and it's about recognizing the contributions and value each of us brings to this team."

Will started with his own acknowlededgment. "I'd like to acknowledge Jenna for her leadership on the recent website project. Your dedication has not only driven the project to success but has also uplifted your team. Thank you, Jenna."

Encouraged, several team members followed, each taking a moment to express gratitude for their colleagues' support, hard work, and positive impact. From celebrating milestones to thanking someone for lending a listening ear during tough times, the room filled with a sense of unity and appreciation.

Then, from the speakerphone, a voice rang out, clear and cheerful.

"Hi, everyone, it's Jake! I just had to dial in from vacation for this. First up, big shout out to Alex for covering for me while I'm away, and to Sam for helping me with that . . . big problem, last week. You guys rock!" Everyone laughed at Jake's reference to a "big problem."

After Jake's turn, the atmosphere in the room was one of emotional warmth and mutual respect. It was then that Shera, who had been quietly observing the proceedings, tentatively raised her hand. "Can I say something?" she asked. Will nodded, encouraging her to speak.

"I just want to thank all of you for letting me be a part of this meeting. It's been incredibly insightful to see how much you all genuinely care for and appreciate each other. It's clear that this company isn't just about work; it's about building a community. Thank you for welcoming me into this space today."

Her words, simple yet profound, resonated deeply, reinforcing the sense of community and shared Purpose that Will had sought to cultivate within his team. As the meeting adjourned, there was a shared feeling of gratitude and connection, a testament to the power of acknowledgements in shaping a positive and inclusive company culture.

As the room cleared and the hum of conversation dwindled, Will and Shera found a quiet corner to catch up.

"That was something, wasn't it?" Shera began, a note of admiration in her voice. "Jake dialing in from his vacation just to make acknowledgements. It really says something about the culture you've built here."

Will smiled, accepting the compliment. "Yeah, that was cool, wasn't it? It's happened a few times, and it always shocks me. I suppose it's about being there for each other, no matter where we are."

As they continued to discuss the meeting's highlights, Will steered the conversation towards a deeper insight. "Did you notice how the meeting itself was structured around our three Tenets?" he asked.

Shera paused, reflecting on the meeting's flow and content. "Now that you mention it, yes. Remind me what your core Tenets are? I assume you know them by heart?" She laughed, knowing that of course he did.

Will smiled. "Attracting and retaining exceptional people, building remarkable products and experiences, and striving for operational excellence."

"Right," Shera said. The realization seemed to spark an even greater interest in her, highlighting the intentionality behind the meeting's organization. "I can see how the meeting was organized against those. The first parts were focused on the team, the second on the work, and the third was a pretty frank discussion on the financial performance of the business."

As their conversation wound down, Shera extended her gratitude. "Thank you, Will, for allowing me to attend today. I'm excited to take what I've learned back to my team. I've got a lot of work to do to create our PVTV, and I hope it's OK if I reach out when I get stuck."

"Absolutely, ask at any time," Will said. "I'm such a big fan of a company building out their PVTV, but most importantly, of them living it each day. I'll mostly be curious with how you execute on it after the hard work of creating it."

—

On the morning of the PVTV Workshop, Shera and Megan decided to ride together. Megan picked Shera up, and they swung by the office to load Megan's car up on all the supplies they would need for the day: Dry erase markers, Post-it notes (big and small), tape, pads, pens, and lots and lots of candy.

The place they'd be meeting was about twenty minutes from the office, just on the outskirts of the city. It was an old-style arcade that had been converted into a conference/meeting venue.

"So, you're saying that Will's company used this place for one of their big meetings?" Megan asked Shera as she pulled into the parking lot.

"Apparently so. In fact, I believe they had their PVTV Workshop here," Shera said. It had been almost a month since Shera had attended Will's company meeting, and she'd worked diligently to prepare for this day.

After checking in with the receptionist, they entered the main meeting space. It was just what they needed: a large, open room with a dozen or so tables so that they could break the company into teams. Each table had a corresponding rolling whiteboard.

Megan began to put the supplies on each table, including a

package of large marshmallows and toothpicks. "So you're still not going to tell me what the marshmallows are for, huh?" She asked Shera.

"Nope. *Remember*, you're participating in this, so I can't give you an inside scoop!"

"Well, I don't see a firepit anywhere, so I can't imagine they're for s'mores . . . " Megan said.

Shera laughed, "No, and even if it were, you'd burn yourself up trying to roast marshmallows with toothpicks!"

"Fair enough," Megan said, laughing as well. "And the nameplates I put at each position . . . I can see that you properly mixed everyone up, didn't you?"

Shera smiled. "Yes, I thought it would be important also to use this time to get people to meet their team members in other departments – "

"Plus," Megan jumped in, "I would imagine you'd get less 'group think' or, I guess you might call it, 'division think,' by not having a bunch of people who work together all the time collaborating on these ideas."

"You got it. Maybe *you* should be running this company . . . "

"No thanks! I don't want that kind of responsibility . . . yet," Megan said with a smirk. "Anything else I can do to help? Otherwise, I see a Ms. Pac-Man calling my name . . . "

"Knock yourself out. I have to run through what I'm going to say to kick things off anyway," Shera said.

Shera had the game plan down for the workshop, and she wanted to make sure to kick things off on the right foot. She had given the company very little detail about what they'd be doing, simply calling the meeting "Company-wide PVTV Meeting," knowing full well most of them wouldn't know a PVTV if it walked up to them on the sidewalk.

As was her custom, she began rehearsing what she'd say.

—

"Welcome, everyone. Today, we're not just in an arcade, but at a turning point for SalesLive. We're here to craft our Purpose, Vision, Tenets, and Values — our PVTV. This isn't just about strategy; it's about understanding our 'why' and building a culture that reflects it."

Shera's gaze swept across the room. "This process is about much more than defining corporate jargon. It's about digging deep to find the essence of what makes SalesLive unique. Our 'why' is the soul of our business, the reason each of us gets up in the morning excited to come to work. It's about creating an environment where we don't just meet goals, but exceed them through shared passion and commitment."

She paused for a moment, letting her words sink in. "Today, in this unconventional setting, we break free from the confines of a traditional boardroom mentality. We're surrounded by creativity and innovation, symbolized by these arcade games. Let's use this energy to think outside the box, to be bold and imaginative in defining our PVTV. What we establish today will become the cornerstone of our culture, guiding SalesLive into a future where we not only succeed but thrive."

George, with a thoughtful expression, was the first to speak.

"Shera, how do we ensure that our PVTV genuinely resonates with every team member, regardless of their role?"

"It starts with inclusion, George. Our PVTV must be co-created, ensuring every voice is heard and reflected. It's about shared beliefs and common goals," Shera said.

Paige, a member of the Technology team, looked up from her notes and asked, "In terms of our company's legacy, how do we envision our PVTV guiding us through future challenges?"

Shera said, "Our PVTV is our compass, Paige. It will guide us not just in smooth seas but also through storms. It's about maintaining our course and values, no matter the challenge."

Megan asked, "How will our PVTV influence our product design and customer experience?"

Shera, knowing that Megan was asking more for the team to hear the answer than for herself, responded, "Our products are our message to the world, Megan. They should embody our PVTV, demonstrating our Values and Vision to our customers through what we create and deliver."

The room, illuminated by the arcade's playful ambiance, now

buzzed with a deeper understanding. They were not just defining words; they were shaping the heart and soul of SalesLive.

There were a few more questions, but mainly, people just wanted to get going. The team was broken up into eight tables of ten. Shera then told the group, "The first thing we're going to do is have a little friendly competition. In just a second, I'm going to start a five-minute timer on my watch. Whichever team builds the tallest structure from the marshmallows and toothpicks on their table wins. Ready . . . set . . . go!"

Instantly, the room burst into a flurry of activity. Each table, now a mini battlefield of creativity, saw hands diving into marshmallow bags and toothpick boxes. Laughter and playful banter filled the air as teams strategized and collaborated.

Shera walked around, observing the chaos with a smile. At one table, a group was attempting an ambitious pyramid structure; their faces a picture of intense concentration. Another table had divided tasks with military precision, but their tower wobbled dangerously. A third group seemed more focused on eating the marshmallows than building.

She noticed Vijay's team constructing something that looked more like a sculpture than a stable structure. George's team, on the other hand, was methodically building a surprisingly tall and slender tower, their engineering skills coming to the fore.

The five-minute mark approached and the teams started to scramble even more. Shera could see some structures collapsing under their own ambition, while others stood surprisingly sturdy.

Finally, the timer beeped. "Time's up!" Shera called out, silencing the room. She walked around with a measuring tape, carefully assessing each structure. The room was filled with a mix of anticipation and laughter.

The pyramid team's structure was impressive but not the tallest. Vijay's sculptural masterpiece was visually stunning but fell short in height. It was George's team's slender tower that stood the tallest, albeit slightly leaning.

"And the winner is . . . George's team!" Shera announced. The team erupted in cheers, while the others playfully groaned and applauded.

Shera's eyes twinkled with satisfaction as she looked at her vibrant team, now more connected and energized than before. After everyone settled down, Shera gathered everyone's attention.

Shera said, "Great job, everyone! I hope you all had fun with this exercise. But let's take a moment to reflect on why we did this. This wasn't just about building towers with marshmallows and toothpicks. It was a metaphor for how we work together at SalesLive."

She paused, ensuring she had everyone's attention.

"First, it was about creativity and innovation. There are no set instructions on how to build a successful company. We need to think outside the box, be bold, and sometimes take unconventional paths to reach our goals."

Shera walked slowly among the tables, making eye contact with her team members.

"It also highlighted the importance of collaboration and communication. You had to work together, share ideas, and build on each other's strengths to create something stable and strong. That's exactly how we need to operate as a team at SalesLive."

She gestured towards the different structures around the room.

"And lastly, it showed that failure is a part of the process. Some structures didn't hold up, and that's okay. We learn, we adapt, and we try again. It's about resilience and persistence. Our journey in defining and living our PVTV will be similar. We might face setbacks, but it's our collective effort and determination that will lead us to success."

The room nodded in understanding, the playful exercise now seen in a new light.

"Uh, Shera," said a young man toward the back, "it's cool if we eat these marshmallows now, right?"

Everyone laughed, and Shera said, "Of course, Billy, eat away."

Shera then turned on the overhead projector, and an agenda slide popped up. It read:

1. **Setting the Stage**
2. **Values**
3. **Purpose**

4. Vision
5. Tenets

While the order of PVTV had Purpose first, Will had suggested that she start by working with the team to develop their Values, as this would lead easily into the Purpose discussion. She walked the team through how the rest of the day would go, answered a few questions, and then moved into the Values exercise.

"First, we're going to take a step towards defining our team's Values," she began, her voice clear and encouraging. "We'll start with a brainstorming exercise that I believe will help us uncover what truly matters to us as a team.

"We'll break into groups of four or five people, with two groups per table. Each person will share with their group someone they most admire and respect. It could be someone you know personally or someone you know of."

Shera paused to ensure everyone was following. "Discuss what traits these individuals have that you hope to embody. Feel free to share a story if applicable. It's through our stories that we can really understand the impact of these traits."

After a moment of letting the instructions sink in, she continued, "Once everyone has had a chance to share, I want you to identify the common themes or traits across each story that resonate most with your group. Choose someone to write down one trait per Post-it note."

The room buzzed conversations began to flow. Laughter and nods of agreement filled the air as stories were shared, from personal heroes to historical figures, each tale highlighting admirable traits such as resilience, empathy, creativity, and integrity.

As the exercise progressed, each group engaged in lively discussions, debating which traits stood out and why they were important. Post-it notes in vibrant colors began to populate the tables, each one representing a Value that someone in the group aspired to embody.

Finally, Shera called everyone back together. "Now, let's regroup and share the Values you've identified with your table. If you see similar traits, consolidate them. This is how we'll begin to see what our collective Values might look like."

One by one, the groups shared their findings, often discovering overlaps in Values such as honesty, innovation, teamwork, and respect. The room was a collaborative hub, with team members actively listening, engaging, and refining the list of Values that were beginning to form the backbone of their team's identity.

As the exercise concluded, each team handed Shera a stack of Post-its with their group's Values on them. Shera told the team they could take a ten-minute break while she organized them.

Shera then began meticulously organizing the colorful Post-its on the wall, each bearing a Value her team identified as core to their identity. Thirteen distinct Values stood in a row: a vibrant testament to the diversity of thought and aspiration within the room.

After everyone came back to their tables, Shera said, "Let's discuss each of these Values to ensure we all understand what they truly mean to us."

Picking a Post-it, Shera started. "For example, 'Innovation' — to us, it's not just about coming up with new ideas but also about being fearless in questioning the status quo and being persistent in finding better solutions." Nods and murmurs of agreement rippled through the room, and a few team members weighed in on what Innovation meant to them.

After ensuring clarity and shared understanding around each Value, Shera introduced the next exercise. "Now, we'll each have 2 'ups' and 2 'downs.' You can move a Value up the wall — the height of one Post-it — to signify its importance or down if you feel other Values should take precedence. Remember, you can move one Post-it up twice or two Post-its up once, and the same for moving them down.

"And, I'd like everyone to decide on their two 'ups' and two 'downs' before anyone moves a Post-it; otherwise, you'll end up influencing each other too much as the Post-its begin moving," she explained.

The team engaged with the exercise thoughtfully, each member approaching the wall to adjust the Post-its according to their personal convictions and the prior discussions.

By the end of the exercise, four Values rose to the top: Dependability, Hard-Working, Trustworthy, and Respect. These Values, now elevated both literally and metaphorically, drew nods and smiles of acknowledgement from the team.

Shera walked to the whiteboard at the front of the room and wrote the four Values in big, block letters. She turned back to her team and said, "These are the Values that have emerged as our top priorities: Dependability, Hard-Working, Trustworthy, and Respect. Do these feel right to everyone?"

The team responded with enthusiasm, sharing examples that reinforced their agreement. "Dependability is crucial for us; knowing we can rely on each other makes all the difference," one team member shared. Another added, "And respect—it's the foundation of how we interact, regardless of our roles or opinions."

Shera then shifted to a new exercise, leading the group through a discussion on each Value to "pressure-test" them, as she put it. "Megan is going to pass out a paper with four questions on it that I want you to ask in terms of each of these four Values. We need to make sure these Values are right for us."

The questions, which Will had helped her devise, were:

- *What does this Value mean to us?*
- *What actions can we connect to this Value (within the team, with customers/partners, etc.)?*
- *How could this Value be misinterpreted?*
- *How will we measure this Value?*

Shera gave them 20 minutes for this part of the exercise. When done, she asked for some examples of what was discussed.

"For Dependability," Shera started, scanning the room for

volunteers, "can someone articulate what this Value means to us as a team?"

A hand went up, and Alex responded, "Let's see what we have here . . . Dependability is about reliability and consistency. It's showing up, delivering on promises, and being a steady force others can count on, whether it's meeting deadlines or supporting a teammate in need."

Encouraged by the thoughtful answer, Shera moved on to the next Value. "Thank you, Alex. Now, for Trustworthiness, what actions can we connect to this Value, both within the team and in our interactions with customers and partners?"

Jenna said, "Actions reflecting Trustworthiness include honest communication, protecting confidential information, and acting with integrity in every decision. It's about building a foundation of trust through our actions every day."

With the conversation flowing smoothly, Shera posed a question about the third Value. "Hard-working is crucial for us. How could this Value be misinterpreted by others?"

"There's a risk," Kevin said, standing, "of Hard-Working being seen as merely logging long hours, rather than focusing on productivity and the quality of our work. We need to ensure it's understood as delivering our best, efficiently and effectively."

"I'm so glad you said that," Shera said. "The last thing we want is a culture that is focused primarily on seeing how hard we can push each other. We want to work hard, but also smart."

Lastly, Shera directed the group's attention to Respect. "How will we measure this Value within our team and in our broader organizational culture?"

Lily, sitting at the table directly in front of Shera, said, "Our group had a tough time with this one, but ultimately decided that Respect can be measured through feedback on our work environment, how well we listen to and value each other's opinions, and through the inclusivity of our team dynamics. It's about creating a space where everyone feels valued and heard."

Shera nodded appreciatively at each contribution. "These insights are invaluable. By defining, connecting actions to, understanding potential misinterpretations of, and measuring our core Values, we're laying the groundwork for a culture that embodies Dependability, Trustworthiness, Hard-Working, and Respect. Let's continue to hold these discussions and reflect on our Values as we move forward, ensuring they are not just words, but principles that guide our actions and decisions every day."

Shera clicked a button on her laptop and the next slide said, "Purpose." Checking her watch, Shera said, "OK, I'm going to keep us moving for a bit and see how far we can get before lunch is delivered."

"So you know, the next step with completing the Values we just developed will be for the Leadership Team to meet independently and work on phrasing the Values within the sentence, 'We believe in . . .' But for now, we can move on to our Purpose."

"But first, let's kick things off with a bit of fun!" Shera announced, her voice capturing the room's attention. "We're going to have another competition between the tables. It's called the Brand Quiz, and here's how it works." She gestured to the pieces of paper being distributed among the tables by Megan, each sheet listing 12 brands alongside 12 Purpose statements. "Your task is to match each brand with its Purpose statement by drawing a line between them. The table with the most correct answers wins!"

Facilitator instructions for this activity on page 168.

The room instantly buzzed with a competitive spirit, each table huddling closely, debating and drawing lines with a mix of strategy and guesswork. Laughter and light-hearted disputes filled the room as each team strived to outdo the others.

After ten minutes, Shera called for time. The room fell silent with anticipation as she reviewed the results. "And the winners are . . . Table Four, with an impressive eight correct matches!" she announced. Cheers erupted from Table Four, their faces beaming with pride and triumph.

"Any reflections on this exercise?" Shera asked.

Jake leaned forward, a puzzled expression on his face as he held up their answer sheet. "I really thought Spotify's Purpose was to entertain the world, not to unlock the potential of human creativity," he admitted, scratching his head.

Mia, sitting across from Jake, nodded in agreement. "It's easy to see how Spotify and Netflix could be confused. Netflix's Purpose to entertain the world seemed to fit both," she added, looking around the table for nods of agreement.

Liam, who had been quiet, chimed in with a bit of insight. "It's fascinating how specific each Purpose is, yet they're all about impacting lives positively. Like, we matched Patagonia with 'To refresh the world in mind, body, and spirit,' thinking it was about their environmental focus. But their actual Purpose, 'We're in business to save our home planet,' is so much more direct and powerful."

"You're right, Liam," Shera said. "Each brand's Purpose is carefully chosen to reflect not just what they do, but why they do it and the impact they aim to have. It's a powerful reminder of the importance of Purpose in guiding a brand's actions and decisions."

Emma asked, "So, for brands like Lego, their Purpose 'To inspire and develop the builders of tomorrow' isn't just about playing with bricks. It's about inspiring creativity and problem-solving in kids?"

Shera smiled, nodding. "Exactly, Emma. It's about looking beyond the product itself to the effect it has on individuals and communities. That's the essence of Purpose. It's not just a statement; it's a commitment to making a positive impact in every way possible."

Shera then transitioned to the heart of the session. "Now, let's delve into our Purpose. As we've discussed, Purpose is not just about what we do; it's about why we do it. It's the driving force that guides us, the light that illuminates our path forward. It's about making a meaningful impact, not just within our company, but in our community, and the world at large.

"Purpose is what gives our work significance," Shera continued. "It's why we're all here today. It's about asking ourselves why our company exists, what positive impact we aim to have, and how we can achieve that through our actions, our services, and our engagement with the community."

She clicked the remote, and the presentation slide changed to display three questions:

- *Why are we / our community / the world better because our company exists?*
- *What impact do we want to have on our team / our community / the world?*
- *How can we make a positive impact through how we treat each other, the work we do and services we produce, and the way we engage with our community?*

The room grew contemplative, the weight of the questions sinking in. A few hands raised, and team members began to ask questions, seeking clarification and offering reflections. "How do we balance our Purpose with our need for profit?" one asked. Another queried, "Can our Purpose evolve as we grow, or is it something that remains constant?"

Shera answered each question thoughtfully, emphasizing that Purpose and profit can coexist harmoniously, and that while the core of a Purpose is enduring, the ways in which it manifests can evolve over time. "Our Purpose should be our compass," she concluded, "guiding us in decisions, actions, and the impact we strive to create."

Sensing the room's anticipation for the next phase, Shera

explained that next they'd be doing the "Why?" exercise. "This exercise is rooted in the principle that by continuously asking 'Why?' and peeling back the layers of surface-level reasoning and get to the core of our Purpose," she explained. "It's about challenging ourselves to think beyond the obvious and explore the deeper motivations behind why our business exists."

Seeing a few puzzled looks around the room, Tom, one of the participants, raised his hand. "Could you give us a simple example of how asking 'Why?' might work?"

Shera nodded, pleased with the question. "Sure, Tom. Let's say our initial Purpose statement is 'Our Purpose is to sell high-quality furniture.' If we ask 'Why?' we might say it's because we want to enhance people's living spaces. Ask 'Why?' again, and we could say it's to improve people's quality of life through their environment. Keep asking 'Why?' and we may discover our true Purpose is to foster a sense of comfort, belonging, and happiness in people's homes."

Shera continued, "So, you'll start with a basic Purpose statement on your index card. Then, you'll pass it to the person on your left, and that person asks 'Why?' to your statement. Along the way, you're diving deeper into the heart of what drives our company. This iterative process not only helps us understand our own Purpose better but also encourages us to think critically about the impact we want to have."

She did some quick math, looking at the tables, and said, "Let's have every third person write the initial statement. And then after the cards go to three or four people, each asking 'Why?'

then collaborate as a team to come up with one final Purpose statement to present."

Shera then set a timer on her watch for 45 minutes.

—

About halfway through the 45 minutes, Shera began moving around the room, observing the teams intensely discussing their index cards. She noticed a common theme: many were stuck on surface-level descriptions of what their company does, struggling to move beyond the tangible to the intangible aspects of their Purpose.

Approaching one group, she overheard them debating a statement. "Our Purpose is to provide marketing services," one member read aloud, a note of frustration in his voice. Shera leaned in, her expression thoughtful. "But why do you provide those services?" she asked. "What change are you seeking to make in the world through your work?"

The group fell silent for a moment, considering her question. Shera encouraged them further, "Think about the impact of your work on our clients' businesses and, ultimately, on their customers. What deeper need are you fulfilling?"

She moved to another table, where the team was similarly challenged. "Our Purpose is to develop sales software, right?" a team member asked, looking up at Shera expectantly. Shera smiled, challenging them. "And why is that important? How does your software change the lives of those who use it?"

Shera continued her rounds, guiding each team with questions that prompted deeper reflection, helping them see beyond their products or services. She emphasized the importance of connecting their work to a larger impact on society, the environment, or the way people interact with each other within the company.

Eventually, her timer went off, and she said, "As soon as you turn in your Purpose statement to me, you're free to eat lunch!" This seemed to add the right motivation to the team, as group after group began handing their Post-its to her. Once she had each table's statement, she began writing them on the whiteboard.

After she had all the statements on the whiteboard, she grabbed her own lunch off the buffet and joined a table filled with the sounds of conversations and laughter. After finishing her meal, she moved towards the whiteboard at the front of the room.

"Hey, everyone, feel free to keep eating while we work on these Purpose statements," she said. The room fell silent, turning their attention to her. In front of the whiteboard, filled with various Purpose statements, she asked for their thoughts on which of the statements stood out to them the most.

Colleagues began to raise their hands, sharing their thoughts and building on each other's ideas. The discussion centered around the theme of empowering customers, with each suggestion adding clarity to their collective Purpose.

After a collaborative effort, a final statement emerged as the consensus: "To empower our customers to achieve their goals, by providing innovative and tailored software solutions with excellence and passion." The room agreed unanimously that this statement best captured their Purpose.

Shera agreed with the statement, but a suggestion Will had made was poking at her: *Purpose statements should be short and powerful* . . .

"Before we lock this Purpose statement in, let me ask this question . . . why do we need the last part, 'by providing innovative and tailored solutions with excellence and passion?' Besides the fact that once we have our PVTV created, we'll all, at some point down the road, be asked to memorize it, so brevity might be important to you." This prompted laughter from the group.

"But in all seriousness, I love the power of 'Our Purpose is to empower our customers to achieve their goals,' and then in our Vision will talk about how we do that. Do you think that statement can stand on its own?" she asked.

The room fell into a thoughtful silence as her question hung in the air. After a moment, a team member named Steve spoke up.

"I think you're onto something, Shera. The first part is powerful and direct. It tells us why we're here. The details of how we achieve that Purpose can indeed be captured in our Vision," he said, nodding in agreement.

Another colleague, Alex, chimed in, "I agree with Steve. Keeping the Purpose statement focused on the 'why' makes it memorable and impactful. It's the essence of what drives us."

As the discussion evolved, a new consideration surfaced. Maya, one of the creative team members, raised a point that resonated with everyone. "While I love the focus on our customers, I remember some of our other discussions highlighted the importance of supporting each other. Shouldn't our Purpose also reflect how we intend to support and uplift our own team members?"

The suggestion sparked a new wave of conversation. The team debated how to incorporate this internal focus without diluting the statement's power.

After several minutes, Shera summarized the consensus. "So, we're saying our Purpose could be dual-focused. Not only are we here to empower our customers to achieve their goals, but we're also committed to fostering a supportive environment for our team. It's about external and internal empowerment."

Steve nodded. "Exactly. It's about striking a balance. Our Purpose should reflect both our commitment to our customers and to each other."

The team agreed, and after a few more tweaks, they landed on a revised Purpose statement that captured both elements succinctly. "Our Purpose is to empower our team and customers to achieve their goals."

There was a collective sense of satisfaction in the room. Shera smiled. "I think we've got it. This encapsulates who we are and what we stand for, both externally and internally. Thank you, everyone, for your thoughtful contributions. I'm really impressed with how much progress we've made already!"

Shera nodded towards Megan, who stood up and said, "Okay,

team, let's shake off the post-lunch lethargy and get a bit of fresh air. We're going for a short walk through downtown. A little movement will do wonders for our creativity and focus."

The group, initially surprised, welcomed the break. They gathered their belongings and followed Megan out of the workshop space, trailing behind her. The small downtown area, with its quaint shops and cafes, provided a picturesque backdrop for their walk. The air was crisp, and the slight bustle of the streets added a lively energy to their group.

As they meandered through the streets, laughter and light conversation filled the air. The walk was not just a physical break but a mental one as well, allowing everyone to relax and momentarily step away from the intensity of the workshop.

Meanwhile, Shera used this opportunity to gather her thoughts. The break in the workshop the walk provided was not just beneficial for the participants, but invaluable for her as well. She found a quiet bench and sat down, pulling out her notebook.

She reflected on the morning's discussions, the feedback she had received, and the progress the group had made so far. With a few hours left in their time together, she wasn't sure they'd be able to get through Vision and Tenets, but if she could keep them focused . . .

Just then, Megan returned with the group. The walk seemed to have done the trick, as they were more energetic, laughing and bantering as they made their way to the tables.

After everyone was settled, Shera kicked things off again.

"We're now going to focus on what a company's Vision truly is," Shera began, her voice clear and engaging. "Vision is about painting a picture of where we aim to be in the future. It's not just any picture, though — it's our three- to five-year goal, the roadmap we're crafting for our future."

The slide behind her illuminated her points:

- Vision is more tangible than the Purpose and needs to be revisited every 3-5 years
- It's ambitious yet feasible
- Achieving our Vision moves us closer to our Purpose
- It complements, not conflicts with, our Purpose
- Must be trackable

Shera paused, allowing the information to sink in. A hand raised from the group: Tom, a thoughtful member of the team.

"Can you clarify what you mean by 'Vision is more tangible than Purpose'?" Tom asked.

"Of course." Shera turned slightly to address him directly. "While our Purpose serves as our north star, guiding why we do what we do, our Vision is the company we aspire to be. Vision is connected more directly to the work we do and our actual business."

Another question came from Maya, who's always keen on details: "How do we ensure our Vision doesn't conflict with our Purpose?"

"A great question, Maya. We can do that by keeping our Purpose at the core of every decision, including how we craft our Vision. Every aspect of our Vision should align with and advance our

Purpose, ensuring they complement rather than conflict with each other." Shera's explanation sparked nods of understanding around the room.

Feeling the group's growing understanding and enthusiasm, Shera transitioned to the next phase. "Now, I'd like us to spend the next 30 minutes working together on crafting our Vision statement." She clicked to the next slide, presenting a new set of questions for the team to ponder:

- *Think about our company today . . . what are things you'd like us to improve or build upon?*
- *What kind of company do we ultimately aspire to become?*
- *What does success look like in three years along that journey? In five years?*
- *What would make you proud of our company and happy to have helped us get there?*
- *Consider specific size, market reputation, or important attributes.*

"Choose someone to take notes on your whiteboard," Shera instructed, her gaze sweeping across the room to meet the eyes of her colleagues. "These questions are your guide. Let's dive deep into what our future can look like."

After ten minutes, Shera moved quietly among the groups, her ears catching the vibrant discussions that filled the room. She noted the dedication in their voices but also realized a common confusion among many teams.

Listening in, she heard one group enthusiastically list objectives like innovative product development, customer service excellence, and sustainability practices. While commendable, these goals mirrored Tenets more closely than a Vision.

Intervening gently, Shera suggested, "These goals are impressive, indeed. But remember, Tenets are the principles we'll use to achieve our Vision. Let's think bigger. When we achieve these Tenets, what will our company look like in three or five years?"

Confusion was evident as the group exchanged glances, struggling with the conceptual shift. They weren't alone. Another team faced a similar predicament, their whiteboard filled with detailed but operational milestones.

Shera, noticing their bewilderment, offered further insight: "Envision our Tenets in action. What impact have they created? How has our company transformed? That's the future state our Vision should describe."

Shera decided to make an announcement as she was sure many teams were struggling with this same issue. "Everyone, listen up for just one second. I want you to keep in mind that our Vision isn't merely a list of achievements; it's a depiction of our future success, shaped by our Tenets. Consider how our efforts have changed us. I want you to literally think of what we look like as a company three to five years from now."

With Shera's encouragement, the teams dug deeper. As the session advanced, moments of understanding and clarity started to break through among the challenged teams. With Shera's continuous support and direction, they gradually began to articulate Visions that captured not only their objectives but also who they aspired to become.

Once all the Vision statements were crafted, Shera turned her attention to the collective task at hand. She asked each table to share their Vision, creating an atmosphere of anticipation and collaboration. As the groups presented, Shera meticulously noted each statement on the board, ensuring every idea was visible and considered.

The first group stood up, their spokesperson confidently articulating their Vision: "To innovate and lead in customer-centric solutions, transforming the way small to medium-sized businesses thrive."

Shera wrote it down, nodding appreciatively. "That's ambitious, focusing on transformation and leadership. How do we see ourselves achieving this in the context of sales professionals?" she prompted, sparking a discussion on the practical steps and challenges involved in reaching such a transformative goal.

The next group shared their Vision: "In five years, we aim to revolutionize the sales industry by being at the forefront of technology and service, making us the go-to partner for growth-minded businesses."

Shera added this to the board, turning to the group. "This places a strong emphasis on technology and partnership. It's forward-thinking, but let's consider how it aligns with our core focus on sales professionals specifically," she observed, encouraging the group to consider the specificity of their target audience and the realistic path to becoming a "go-to partner."

Finally, the third table presented a Vision that immediately resonated with the room: "To be the top choice for sales professionals of small to medium-sized businesses in five years."

Shera wrote it on the board, and a sense of agreement filled the room. "This statement is direct and clearly aligned with our Purpose," Shera reflected "It speaks directly to our target audience and sets a measurable timeline."

The discussion that followed was rich with constructive feedback and perspectives. One team member, Jake, pointed out, "The first two Visions are inspiring, but they might be a bit broad. This last one, however, is specific and aligns perfectly with our discussions on Purpose."

Another colleague, Lila, added, "It's ambitious yet achievable. Focusing on being the top choice highlights our commitment to excellence and differentiates us in the market."

As the debate unfolded, it became clear that the third Vision struck the best balance between ambition and specificity. It encapsulated the team's aspirations in a way that was both challenging and closely tied to its operational strengths and market focus.

Shera, seeing the consensus forming, summarized the sentiment, "This Vision – *To be the top choice for sales professionals of small to medium-sized businesses in five years* – captures our essence and sets a clear direction for our efforts. It's about excellence, focus, and achieving a leadership position that's recognized by our core audience.

"While we're about to move on to our Tenets – how we plan to achieve our Vision – I did want to point out that the Leadership

Team will be spending time mapping out how we will measure our Vision. It's critical that, as we move forward, we are able to gauge how well we are progressing toward our Vision," she said.

"We're going to start building out our Tenets by going through an exercise called the 'Kitchen Sink.' This is where we throw everything but the kitchen sink at our problems and Vision.

"The objective here," she continued, "is to brainstorm all possible actions, ideas, and strategies that could help us achieve our Vision. Imagine a whiteboard in front of us that we want to fill with every thought, no matter how big or small, that could move us toward our goal."

Tom, intrigued by the brainstorming aspect, raised his hand to ask, "Do we focus on any specific areas, or is everything on the table?"

"Great question, Tom," Shera said. "Everything is on the table. Whether it's improving our products, enhancing customer experience, or internal processes, we want to capture it all. This is about exploring every avenue without restrictions."

Emma, who had been nodding along to Shera's explanation, then asked, "How do we ensure we're not just throwing out ideas but actually creating a plan we can act on?"

Shera smiled at Emma's insightful question. "That's where the next step comes in. After our brainstorm, we'll review all the ideas and categorize them into key themes. This helps us transition from a wide array of ideas to a focused set of strategies that are directly tied to our Tenets. It's about finding the actionable steps within our creative storm.

"In fact," she went on, "by the end of this exercise, we'll have a clearer understanding of the specific actions and principles that will guide us toward achieving our Vision, laying a solid foundation for our Tenets. You've got 20 minutes, so let's get started."

The team then got to work, filling up the whiteboards near their tables with ideas ranging from basic tactics to big, strategic concepts. Shera made her way through the room, and even though she knew this would likely be the "easiest" of the exercises she would task them with, she was still pleased with the progress they were making.

After completing the "Kitchen Sink" exercise, with each table having generated a comprehensive list of actions needed to achieve the company's Vision, Shera gathered the team's attention for the next crucial part of the workshop. She introduced the "Why We Failed" exercise, aiming to shift the team's perspective towards embracing failure as a tool for growth and innovation.

"Team, now that we have a clear action plan to reach our Vision, it's time to pivot to something equally important—understanding and embracing failure," Shera explained. "The 'Why We Failed' exercise is designed to help us preemptively identify potential pitfalls and learn how to navigate them."

She continued, "We're going to look at failure differently. Instead of fearing failure, we'll see it as a stepping stone to success. I want each table to think of a scenario where we failed to achieve our

Vision. Then, dive deep into why that happened. Was it a lack of resources? Did we not fully commit to our Tenets? Were there external factors we didn't account for?"

Tom, always curious, raised his hand. "Do we focus on real failures we've experienced, or are we brainstorming potential failures?"

"Great question, Tom," Shera answered. "For this exercise, let's brainstorm potential failures. Think of it as a stress test for our strategy. If we can anticipate where we might stumble, we can prepare and strengthen our approach."

Emma asked, "How detailed should our scenarios be?"

"Detail is good, Emma," Shera said "The more specific we can be about the failure and its causes, the better we can understand how to avoid or overcome it. Think about anything that could derail us from achieving our Vision."

She gave them another 20 minutes for this exercise, and each table got to work, discussing and documenting potential failure scenarios. This process not only illuminated vulnerabilities in their strategies but also fostered a culture of resilience and adaptability. By the end of the exercise, the room was abuzz with constructive conversations on how to preemptively tackle challenges, ensuring that failure, when it did occur, would be a valuable lesson rather than a setback.

As the 20 minutes concluded, Shera observed the focused energy within the room with satisfaction. "Let's come together and share our insights," she announced, her voice cutting through the hum of discussions. "I'm eager to hear the scenarios you've envisioned and how we can navigate potential pitfalls to stay aligned with our Vision."

First to share was a group led by Alex, a detail-oriented analyst known for his critical thinking. "Our table discussed a scenario where we failed due to not fully committing to continuous improvement and learning," Alex began, standing to address the room. "We imagined a project where tight deadlines forced us to prioritize delivery over quality and learning. This led to missed opportunities for innovation and improvement."

He continued, "To overcome this, we propose instituting 'Learning Sprints' as part of our project cycles. These would be periods where the team focuses solely on innovation, skill development, and process improvements. It ensures that even in the busiest times, we dedicate effort to live by our Tenets and move closer to our Vision."

Next, Julia, a project manager with a knack for strategic planning, shared her table's thoughts. "We identified a potential failure stemming from insufficient resources, particularly in the form of skilled personnel," she said. "This could lead us to fall short of our ambitious goals.

"Our solution," Julia added, "involves creating a more dynamic resource allocation model. This model would allow us to quickly shift resources across projects as needed, ensuring that we're always positioned to act on our most critical priorities."

Finally, Marcus, a soft-spoken but insightful member of the R&D team shared a scenario focused on external factors. "We considered the impact of rapid technological change outpacing our product development cycles," he explained. "This could lead to our offerings becoming obsolete before they even reach the market.

"To mitigate this," Marcus proposed, "we could establish a 'Futures Team' tasked with continuously scanning the horizon for emerging technologies and trends. This team would enable us to anticipate changes and adapt our strategies proactively, ensuring we remain at the forefront of innovation."

After a few more teams shared, Shera said, "Great job, everyone. As you know, this exercise isn't about pessimism; it's about preparedness. By embracing the possibility of failure, we become more fearless and innovative in our pursuit of our Vision."

Shera then moved on to the next step of the workshop, asking each team to jot down on Post-Its the action items they believed were crucial for achieving the company's Vision. She encouraged them to pull all the ideas from their "Kitchen Sink" exercise and begin grouping them, and then read through their "Why We Failed" notes to see if anything needed to be added. The teams quickly got to work, scribbling down their thoughts and handing them to Shera when they were finished.

Once all the Post-its were handed in, Shera cut the team loose for a 15-minute break. She then began to organize the myriad of Post-Its into coherent clusters. When the team returned, refreshed and ready for the next challenge, the room buzzed with curiosity about the clusters of Post-Its now neatly arranged on the wall.

Shera called Megan to assist in the next phase. "Megan, could you help divide everyone into four groups?" she asked. Once the teams were organized, Shera unveiled the next phase of their journey towards defining their Tenets.

"Each of these groups of Post-Its," Shera gestured to the wall, "represents a fundamental area we need to focus on to achieve our Vision. They are: having great team members, staying on top of innovation and technology, being known in our industry, and achieving great financial results. Each group will now take one of these themes and work on crafting a Tenet statement that reflects how we can embody these principles in our daily work."

The room was divided, with each group huddling around their assigned theme. The task was clear: distill their thoughts and discussions into a Tenet statement that captured the essence of their area's contribution to the company's Vision. Each group quickly engaged in animated discussions, debating the best way to articulate their insights into concise, impactful statements.

After 30 minutes of intense collaboration, each group was ready to present their Tenet statement. One by one, they shared their work, revealing the depth of thought and commitment to the company's future.

The first group, championing the Value of teamwork, stood up. Their spokesperson, a seasoned team leader named Elena, articulated their Tenet with conviction. "Our Tenet is to cultivate a diverse, skilled, and motivated workforce."

Shera nodded in approval, acknowledging the succinctness and power of the statement. "Well done, Elena. Perhaps the most important thing we can remember going forward is that great team members are the foundation of our success."

The second group, led by a forward-thinking engineer named Raj, focused on the imperative of innovation. "Our Tenet," Raj began, "emphasizes continuous learning, adaptability, and the embrace of cutting-edge solutions to maintain leadership in a rapidly evolving market." This statement was met with nods of agreement, reflecting the team's commitment to staying at the forefront of technology.

"Splendid work on articulating the essence of staying ahead in innovation and technology," Shera praised. "Now, let's make it even more actionable. Can you refine your Tenet to start with 'We will do this by . . . '?"

Raj and his team huddled briefly, buzzing with ideas. Moments later, Raj stood again, ready to present the refined version of their Tenet. "We think we can distill ours to this: We will do this by fostering a culture of perpetual innovation, encouraging every team member to pursue ongoing education and experimentation . . . what do you think?"

Shera nodded appreciatively, recognizing the clarity and directive nature of the revised Tenet. "Excellent, Raj. Your team crushed it."

Then came the third group, which had taken on the challenge of defining the company's industry presence. Their statement was comprehensive but a bit wordy. "We believe in establishing thought leadership, fostering strong networks, and building a reputation for quality and reliability, to be known in our industry," said Sophia.

Shera appreciated the depth of the statement but saw an opportunity to refine it for clarity and impact. "Sophia and team, that's a great start, but I think you can come up with something that captures the spirit of what you are saying without getting too far into the weeds. I'll give your team five minutes to distill what you have down to its essence."

Sophia and her team circled up, and three minutes later she said, "OK, Shera, I think we have it. We will do this by ensuring the great work we do is known across the industry."

Shera, knowing that the Leadership Team would be refining everything that was created, felt like Sophia's team had made enough progress with their statement to move on. "That's great work, team. Now let's go to Kevin's group to see what they came up with."

Kevin stood up and said, "Well, we focused on the importance of financial health, sustainable growth, and value creation for all stakeholders. We recognize that achieving great financial results is crucial for our long-term success and impact."

He looked to Shera for support, and after she nodded, he continued. "And so, the best way we felt this could be written is: We will do this by prioritizing our financial health and stability."

Shera could sense he wasn't confident about their Tenet. "Do you have some concerns about what you came up with?" she asked.

Another member of Kevin's team, Liz, spoke up. "I think we all just felt like it was too basic or something. Don't we need to have more, I don't know, descriptive words or something?"

There was scattered laughter from the team, and Shera, appreciating Liz's concern, said, "That's a great question, Liz, and I should have been more specific about that when we started. In all of this, we're not writing marketing or branding statements that need to have overly embellished or hollow phrases. We want a clear, concise, and specific list of Tenets that will help guide us forward. And I think what you all came up with, 'by prioritizing our financial health and stability,' is perfect."

Shera then wrote the draft of their PVTV on the whiteboard:

Purpose:
Our Purpose is to empower our team and customers to achieve their goals.

Vision:
To be the top choice for sales professionals of small to medium-sized businesses in five years.

Tenets: ('We will do this by . . . ')
- **cultivating a diverse, skilled, and motivated workforce,**
- **fostering a culture of perpetual innovation, encouraging every team member to pursue ongoing education and experimentation,**
- **ensuring the great work we do is known across the industry, and**
- **prioritizing our financial health and stability**

Values (to be written as 'We believe in . . . '):
Dependability, Trustworthiness, Hard Work, and Respect

She stepped back to review the words with the team. She waited a few minutes before saying anything, aware that many were reading and soaking in what they had come up with.

"I have to say," she said, "this feels pretty good! What do you think?" She turned to face the company.

There were a lot of head nods and more than a few smiles.

Jason, a senior developer, was the first to speak up. "I've been with the company for over five years, and this is the first time I've seen our direction and Values laid out so clearly." His voice carried a mixture of surprise and approval. "It's empowering. Knowing our Purpose and how each of us contributes to the Vision . . . it's motivating."

Next, Elena, from the customer service department, shared her thoughts. "This really aligns with what I've always believed about our work," she commented, her eyes scanning the PVTV on the whiteboard. "Especially the part about empowering our team and customers. It's not just about sales; it's about creating value and making a difference. I'm really proud to be part of this."

Then, Raj added, "The focus on innovation and ongoing education resonates with me. It's not just talk; it's a commitment to action, written into our Tenets. It challenges us to keep growing and adapting. That's how we'll achieve our Vision."

Finally, Kevin, summed it up nicely: "Seeing our Values spelled out like this — Dependability, Trustworthiness, Hard-Working, and Respect — it's a powerful reminder of who we are and what we stand for. This entire PVTV framework . . . it's like we've got a roadmap now, not just for the company, but for how we can be our best selves in our work."

Shera couldn't help but feel a new sense of pride in the team, and a new hope inside of her that they just might be able to create something special together.

After a few more people weighed in, Shera looked at her watch. "We're just about out of time," she said, "and I have to say, I couldn't be more proud of how you all came together and worked hard on creating our PVTV. I honestly didn't think we'd get halfway through it today, and yet here we are, with a full first draft of our PVTV!

"The next step in this process will be for your Leadership Team to begin working on refining this statement. And don't worry, they won't change any of the sentiment here. I'll simply be pushing them to keep working to get each aspect of this — in fact, each word —down to its essence. In the end, we want our PVTV to be as clear and concise — and memorizable, don't forget that! — as possible. Sound good?"

More heads nodded, so Shera concluded by saying, "Thanks again everyone, and now, you're free to go. Make sure you grab some snacks for the drive home, and I'll see you all at the office tomorrow."

The team clapped and Shera thought everyone seemed to be in good spirits. Megan, Vijay, and George all came over and expressed how well they thought everything had gone. The four of them stayed after everyone left, cleaning up, reflecting on the day, and talking about next steps. It was the closest that Shera had felt to them in a long time, and she couldn't help but feel that maybe all this trust and Purpose work had fixed everything at SalesLive.

But it didn't take long for her to realize there was a lot more work to be done.

A TLU TEASER FOR
THE PURPOSE PLAYBOOK

This marks the end of Shera's journey to develop her team's PVTV. The next section contains activities to help you develop your team's PVTV.

However, Shera's story does not end here. The execution of any strategic plan, and in particular as it pertains to PVTV, is where all the impact happens. A great plan with no follow-through is worse than having no plan at all.

In the future, Jeff, Megan, and Teresa plan to share best practices and strategies for implementing your PVTV. If you find yourself with a fully developed PVTV and are ready to begin implementing it prior to the publication of that book, here are some options to get started:

- Go to AlwaysLeadWithPurpose.com for more information.
- Read *The Great Team Turnaround*. This book is a great starting point for moving your team forward after developing your PVTV.
- Reach out to us, and we can help you get started!

THE PLAYBOOK

INTRODUCTION

Welcome to *The Purpose Playbook*. This guide is your roadmap to discovering and crafting your team's Purpose, Vision, Tenets, & Values (PVTV). Whether you're a seasoned leader or newly stepping into a facilitation role, these activities are designed to help you navigate the meaningful journey of shaping a culture that's rooted in Purpose and clear Vision.

The Purpose Playbook is more than a manual; it's a catalyst for transformation within your organization. By engaging with this playbook, you're taking a significant step toward creating an environment where every team member feels aligned with and motivated by your shared Purpose and Vision. And as Jeff Hilimire, co-founder of Purpose Group, likes to say, "Not only does our proven, Purpose-driven approach make the world a better place, it also drives higher-than-industry returns for stakeholders You might say it's a win-win-win."

Here's what you can expect:

Foundational Work: Building Team Trust
This section underscores the importance of team cohesion for its success.

Facilitator's Guide: Implementing *The Purpose Playbook*

This section guides facilitators through discussions that unearth a team's core Purpose, breaking each activity down into manageable steps, complete with tips to lead effective and impactful discussions.

Activities: Crafting PVTV for Participants
This section guides participants through discussions and activities to envision the future, establish the principles and Values that will guide your journey, and effectively craft your PVTV.

Case Studies: Learning from Others
Here you'll find examples from other companies that have embarked on this journey. Note: some names of companies may be altered to maintain confidentiality.

Glossary
Lastly, we've included a glossary of terms for quick reference.

We're Here to Help (Literally)
As you embark on this journey, remember that the power of PVTV lies in its ability to unite and inspire your team. Through thoughtful facilitation and a commitment to these principles, you're poised to lead your organization to new heights of Purpose and performance.

Note: While you can certainly jump into this section without reading the first half of this book, we recommend you read Shera's journey in Chapter One and Chapter Two before proceeding. While it isn't necessary, we also recommend that you read The Great Team Turnaround *for more context as you work your way through the examples and activities in the following pages.*

We've tried to make this an all-in-one, figure-it-out-on-your-own resource for you, yet we know there will be times that you might feel confused, stuck, or overwhelmed. With that in mind, we have created the website **AlwaysLeadWithPurpose.com** so you can ask us questions at any point. Over time, we will take those questions and, along with our answers, create a FAQ for the benefit of all of our readers. So, if you need help, please reach out!

The Significance of *The Purpose Playbook*

Using *The Purpose Playbook* is more than a checkbox exercise; it's about sculpting the soul of your business. With **Purpose**, you're defining your reason for being — your "why" — which becomes the gravitational pull for everything you do. **Vision** offers that bright North Star guiding your journey, ensuring everyone's moving in sync. **Tenets** — those tactical steps — become the reliable recipe for making your Vision a reality. And **Values**? They're the DNA, the moral compass shaping your actions.

PVTV isn't just a corporate playbook; it's a commitment to authenticity, unity, and strategic impact. It aligns leaders, employees, and customers under a single banner, driving meaningful growth and building an enduring legacy.

Developing your team's PVTV is no easy task. It takes time, patience, and a trusting leadership team. You'll work with your team over many sessions and through various exercises to develop an authentic and team-supported PVTV statement. This foundational effort is crucial for aligning leaders, employees, and customers under a unifying Purpose. By defining your "why," creating a guiding Vision, setting practical Tenets, and embedding core Values, you can drive meaningful growth and build a lasting legacy.

Remember, the journey to develop your PVTV is as important as the destination. Embrace the process, trust your team, and let this playbook guide you to sculpt the essence of your business.

FOUNDATIONAL WORK

BUILDING TEAM TRUST

Megan and Teresa, longstanding friends and colleagues of Jeff and passionate followers of his work, have read each of the books in the Turnaround Leadership series and have used the PVTV framework in their work. Megan has successfully integrated PVTV into her team leadership practices in the corporate world, while Teresa has woven it into the fabric of Liminist, her executive and team coaching company. Despite their achievements, they felt a gap—a need for more concrete specifics and measurable outcomes. They recognized that Jeff brought a unique magic to PVTV discussions: knowing what "right" looks like and when a team could be pushed to go further. This is an element they aspired to encapsulate in this book.

United by a shared vision, Jeff, Megan, and Teresa met — sometimes in person, other times bridging distances via Zoom, Teams, and Google Meet. Their objective was clear: to craft a playbook that would merge the principles of PVTV from *The Great Team Turnaround* with the grounded, actionable strategies of *The Great Game of Business*.

As they progressed through building the playbook and testing it out in workshops, they realized a crucial component was missing. Enter Wiley's The Five Behaviors® which was developed in partnership with Patrick Lencioni and is based on the *New York Times* best-seller, *The Five Dysfunctions of a Team*. This framework serves as a good gauge to see if your team is truly ready to commit to their Purpose, or if you need to first establish a stronger foundation. While this framework is only briefly referenced in this book, their hope (Jeff's, Megan's, and Teresa's) is that it will guide leaders and teams toward establishing the critical foundation necessary to become a workplace filled with Purpose, clarity, and transparency.

Thus, *The Purpose Playbook* came into being. Through their respective experiences, Jeff, Megan, and Teresa were acutely aware of the challenges leaders face in translating visionary concepts into everyday business practices. And so, the playbook was meticulously designed to facilitate this transition, making it both seamless and impactful.

This playbook symbolizes the power of ideas, collaboration, and a firm belief in a business philosophy that prioritizes Purpose, people, and positive change over mere profit.

Assessing Readiness

Earlier it was mentioned that Jeff, Megan, and Teresa realized a crucial component was missing: company/team readiness. How do you know your company — or a team within your company — is truly ready for *The Purpose Playbook*? How do you know the right team dynamics and timing are in place?

First, consider if your group genuinely forms a "team." A team isn't just a collection of individuals reporting to the same manager; it needs to be a cohesive unit with mutual accountability and Trust, a shared goal and objectives, and collective responsibility for outcomes. If your group doesn't embody these characteristics of a true team, the PVTV process may not yield the expected results.

Using the checklists below, take a moment to check off the readiness characteristics you believe your team has achieved and identify the ones that still need work:

Characteristics of Leadership Readiness

☐ **Leader's Role:** Transformation begins with committed leadership. For a team to reach its full potential, the leader must be genuinely dedicated to fostering teamwork.

☐ **Right Timing:** Consider the timing of implementing the PVTV framework. Avoid starting the process if the team is too new, undergoing significant changes, or if the organization is facing major shifts like mergers or reorganizations.

Characteristics of Team Readiness

☐ **Strategic Conviction:** The team prioritizes shared results through a strategic framework over ad-hoc tactics and personal accomplishments to propel the business forward.

☐ **Empowered to Drive Change:** Everyone has a clear understanding of the company's Purpose and/or the authority to create it, shape it, and deepen this understanding.

☐ **Purposeful Integration:** "Purpose-washing" does not

exist. The team ensures the Purpose Statement is backed by significant actions.

☐ **Actions Speak Louder:** Everyone is ready to embody the PVTV principles in their daily operations and strategic decisions. Again, shared results over personal accomplishments.

☐ **Plumbing Exists to Support:** The operational systems are aligned and prepared to integrate the PVTV into all aspects of the business.

☐ **Unified Pulse and Clear Conviction:** A holistic commitment across all levels, with measurable outcomes and a vibrant organizational culture, indicates readiness.

☐ **Dedication for the Long Haul:** The team recognizes that adopting PVTV is the beginning of a transformative journey, not just a milestone.

In addition to these markers, assess if your leadership team is ready for the heavy lifting that comes with becoming a high-functioning team. This requires a willingness to invest time and energy into the process.

By understanding the nuances of team dynamics and the importance of timing, you can better gauge your readiness for *The Purpose Playbook*. Remember, most strategic frameworks fail due to a lack of depth, vigor, or authenticity. Your leaders must be prepared to infuse real substance into your Purpose, Vision, Tenets, & Values, ensuring they carry the weight and significance they deserve.

Building Team Cohesion: A Prerequisite to PVTV

What to Do if You Do Not Have a Cohesive Team

If you reviewed the team and leadership readiness lists and found areas where your organization or team is not fully aligned, it's crucial to address these gaps before proceeding to the next section. Embarking on the journey to define and live by your PVTV is a transformative step for any team. Ensuring that these team and leadership elements are in place will significantly enhance the effectiveness and impact of the PVTV process.

We recommend addressing the foundational elements of a high-functioning team as highlighted by Patrick Lencioni in his book, *The Five Dysfunctions of a Team*. This includes building trust, engaging in constructive conflict, committing to decisions, holding one another accountable, and focusing on collective results. If your team is struggling in any of these areas or if you've answered "no" to any of the questions in the **Assessing Readiness** section (on page 152), it's vital to pause and address these challenges first. Take the necessary time to work with your team through the foundational activities suggested.

A great tool for addressing these is Wiley's The Five Behaviors® program, which empowers teams to rethink their approach to teamwork and shape new behaviors. The Five Behaviors® was developed in partnership with Patrick Lencioni and is based on the *New York Times* best-seller, *The Five Dysfunctions of a Team*.

As Five Behaviors™ Authorized Partners, our consultants can also guide you through understanding and strengthening these critical aspects of team dynamics, ensuring your team is truly primed for the PVTV journey.

Starting with The Five Behaviors® assessment, team members will gain insights about themselves, others, and their approach to teamwork. These insights are brought to life through a powerful virtual or in-person facilitated experience that addresses the full spectrum of essential cohesive team behaviors.

When teams start with a foundation of vulnerability-based trust, they can be genuinely transparent and honest with one another. From this foundation, team members can channel the power of productive conflict and debate, commit to shared goals, hold each other accountable, and deliver better results—together.

Good luck and don't forget to have fun!

FACILITATOR'S GUIDE

IMPLEMENTING *THE PURPOSE PLAYBOOK*

This section is for facilitators only. Participants can jump directly to the team activities and avoid unnecessary reading.

We highly suggest you designate a facilitator!

This person should be experienced in driving a group to share their voice and explaining instructions while teams complete exercises. You can contact Always Lead With Purpose and we can assist! We can train people in your company or come as a consultant team to facilitate the whole experience as your Purpose Ambassadors. If you can't find an experienced facilitator, you can still use this book to create your PVTV. We've given step-by-step instructions and fun exercises to leverage on your own.

Are you the designated facilitator? Read on!

Before you plan a workshop, please review this guide in its entirety. Also take a moment to familiarize yourself with the terms and terminology found in the Glossary. We encourage you to have the group read the first few story chapters of *The Purpose Playbook* before the workshop, so they know what they are about to embark on.

How to Use This Guide

This playbook has five sections, including:

P — Identifying Your Purpose
V — Envisioning Your Vision
T — Developing Your Tenets
V — Cultivating the Values
PVTV — Putting it All Together

Before you dive into each section, please remember these activities are designed to be interactive and thought-provoking: fostering open dialogue, reflection, and collaboration crucial for shaping your participating team's Purpose, Vision, Tenets, & Values (PVTV).

While the sections are presented in a specific order, they do not need to be delivered sequentially. For example, through extensive testing, we've found that starting with the Core Values section — particularly after reading *The Five Dysfunctions* by Patrick Lencioni or running through The Five Behaviors® exercises with Teresa — maintains vulnerability-based trust.

To build on this foundation, we typically combine working on Purpose with Core Values. This approach takes advantage of participants' open mindsets, creating an environment where they feel good about working together and can dream big. By focusing on Purpose and Core Values first, teams can see the potential of what can be accomplished when they collaborate effectively.

On the other hand, Vision and Tenets are often paired together, as their development requires a different mentality. Here, the focus shifts to rolling up sleeves and defining concrete objectives.

The team concentrates on what they aim to achieve in the next three to five years and uses the flywheel exercise to confirm their commitment to these objectives.

Additionally, if you engage with the flywheel exercise (more on this later in **Developing Your Tenets** on page 180), you may discover the need to refine your Vision statement.

Tailor the sequence to best suit your team's dynamics. Revisit sections as new insights emerge, ensuring the process remains adaptive and relevant to your team's evolving understanding.

Workshop: Prep Day

Break it Down

Decide how you want to run your workshop depending on the amount of time your team is available. We suggest one to two full days, although we know this isn't always feasible. If you decide to break it up over some time, we suggest pairs: Purpose and Values, then Vision and Tenets. These groupings will help teams maintain an understanding of how each section will come together.

The Set Up

In-person

- Create a room that inspires the group to work together. This can be as one single unit or as separate groups in a healthy competition (depending on your people).

- If you have a large team (10+), we suggest breaking into smaller groups so everyone feels comfortable sharing.

- Whiteboards, markers, Post-it notes, tape, TV(s), candy/snacks/water will keep the team focused and make sharing easier.

- Consider incentivizing your group with small prizes, candy, etc., to keep them focused throughout.

- Make sure to schedule breaks throughout the day.

Virtual

- Ship *The Purpose Playbooks* out to your distributed group so they have it before the big day.

- Create a virtual room, and utilize your video chat features like polls, breakout rooms, hand raising, etc.

- Use an online whiteboard on your virtual meeting tool of choice where everyone can share their answers to the exercises.

- Make sure to schedule off-camera breaks throughout the day.

Select the Activities

There are two types of activities provided in each section to cover all types of learners. The workshop exercises for each section consider both auditory and kinesthetic learners. Regardless of what exercise you choose, they will get you to the same objective, so pick what works for your team. You can also do both if you feel the team requires another exercise to really get to the core of what they are trying to achieve.

Final Tips

Know your audience! Some may not be comfortable speaking out in a group setting, so giving the option of using Post-its can go far with quieter team members. Make sure everyone gets a chance to participate. Timebox each exercise to what works best for your workshop; we have added recommended durations for each.

If constructive discussion and conflict seem tough while going through these exercises, stop the conversation and go to the **Building Team Trust** section of this playbook. It may be necessary to work on vulnerability-based trust and conflict exercises first. While pressure testing these exercises, we had groups that were obviously at odds with why their team or company existed. You'll want to read the room and make sure the team is ready for this section of the playbook. **Your team must be unified before this process begins.**

—

Workshop: Day Of

To set yourself up for success, we suggest you consider the following outline before beginning the exercises:

Set Expectations for the Day

Kick it off with a candid discussion on why you are having the workshop. What is happening (or not happening) in your organization that is leading you to run this workshop with your team? Vulnerability and accountability are important here. This isn't time to blame anyone on lost sales or missed timelines. This is the time to inspire and excite the team for what's to come!

Select Some Icebreakers

Our favorite is called "The Marshmallow Tower." You will see it described in most icebreaker idea lists, but also on page 107 of this book.

If you would like to research new or different brainstorming games, we recommend *Gamestorming* by Dave Gray, Sunni Brown, and James Macanufo.

The Marshmallow Tower Icebreaker

What You'll Need

For each team:
- About 20 toothpicks
- Bag of marshmallows

For you:
- Measuring tape to measure the height of the structures
- Method for countdown (it's best if the teams can see it)

Directions

- Start the task by aiming to build the tallest structure that can stand on its own from the table surface to the top of the marshmallow. The structure must not hang or be attached to something else like a chair or ceiling.
- The whole marshmallow needs to sit at the top of the structure. If you cut or eat any part of the marshmallow, your team will be disqualified.
- Your materials include 20 toothpicks and marshmallows. You can use as many or as few of these as you want, but you can't use the paper bag as part of your structure.
- Feel free to break the toothpicks to make your structure.
- You have five minutes for this challenge. At the end of the time, you must not touch or support your structure. Teams still touching their structure when the time is up will be disqualified.
- Make sure everyone understands the rules. It's okay to repeat them a few times. Before starting, check if there are any questions.

Describe the Objectives for the Workshop

Make sure the team knows what needs to be accomplished within the defined time period. Explain *The Purpose Playbook* to your audience. If they pre-read the book, this could be an opportune time to get feedback and reinforce the need for the workshop. If they did not read it, you'll want to provide context to the group on why you're doing the workshop. You'll want to make sure the group is clear on each area before starting the exercises.

Give Them the Game Plan

Explain to the group how the workshop will run, how teams will work together, what materials they have, and provide any necessary rules or ways of working. (Refer to pages 105-107 of the story for details on how Shera did this.)

—

Workshop: Identifying Your Purpose

Definition

Purpose is the core reason an organization exists, beyond making money. It's the driving force that guides your actions and decisions, and helps you define your path. It answers the question, "Why do we get up in the morning?"

Book Reference

On pages 116-124, Shera's team embarks on a journey to define their Purpose. This section illustrates the importance of Purpose in providing direction and motivation for the team, driving them to align their actions with their deeper "why." By identifying their Purpose, Shera's team sets a clear foundation that informs their decisions and inspires their daily efforts, ensuring they remain focused on their ultimate goals and the impact they wish to achieve.

Prep for the Meeting

- Review the definition of Purpose and plan to discuss the definition with your team
- Refer to the story for inspiration or share excerpts that will center your team around the meaning
- Have your brand exercise prepped and ready to kick off before the team begins the activities

Prep for the Selected Activity

There are two exercise types to cover kinesthetic and visual learners. Depending on your audience, you can select one of or both activities.

Uncover the Core (Option A)

This activity is a brainwriting exercise, an idea-generation technique in which participants independently write down their ideas.

What You'll Need

- Index Cards or a virtual whiteboard
- Pens or a digital writing tool
- Downloaded worksheets from this playbook

If you need an example to center the team, try the following:

- 'Our Purpose is to sell high quality furniture.' *If we ask 'Why?'*
- Because we want to enhance people's living spaces. *Ask 'Why?' again,*
- To improve people's quality of life through their environment. *Keep asking 'Why?'*
- To foster a sense of comfort, belonging, and happiness in people's homes."

WORKSHEET - PURPOSE (OPTION A)

ACTIVITY: UNCOVER THE CORE

01 — BRAINWRITING
Creating Why Statements

1. Everyone on the team has a blank index card at the start.

2. Using the notes you took from the group discussion, write your suggestion for the team's Purpose statement on the top line(s) of your index card.)

3. Pass your card to the person next to you. The next person should answer "why" to the statement you wrote on your card, writing it down. (You will answer the card passed to you.)

4. Continue passing the cards around the room until several statements are on each card. Keep going until each card is full or you run out of answers.

02 — GROUP DISCUSSION
When your team is ready, have a volunteer share the statements on the index cards with the rest of the group.

1. Discuss any themes and make those themes visible to the team for the next part of the activity.

2. As a group, examine the various Purpose statements.

3. Discuss recurring keywords, themes, and insights that emerge from these collective reflections. Take note of them on the next page.

4. Start to draft your final Purpose Statements using the space provided on the next page.

CHECKPOINT: This final statement should:
- begin with "Our Purpose is . . . "
- be short and powerful,
- be unattainable (or close to it),
- and it should distinguish the company or team from competitors or other teams.

196

166

Crafting the Future through Dream Headlines (Option B)

This exercise is more visual than the Uncover the Core exercise and helps the team envision their Purpose-driven future accomplishments. If you do both exercises, this one is a great way to pressure test what you created in Uncover the Core. Note that teams may want access to images or magazine clippings to create a press release example, yet it is not required. As the exercise progresses, make sure outcomes are visible to all participants.

What You'll Need
- Paper or digital document platforms for writing
- Pens or a digital writing tool
- Downloaded worksheets from this playbook

Kicking off the Purpose Workshop

Use the prep work to ready the team for the activities. Review the definition of Purpose, referencing Shera's story.

First, create some healthy competition with a Warm-up activity, using the "Match the Logo" activity (Worksheet located on page 193).

Match the Logo Warm-up Activity Instructions:

1. Present teams with the brand logos and statements, and ask them to connect the correct statement with the correct logo.
2. Whichever team finishes first with all correct matches wins! (Review using the answers on the next page)
3. Discuss with the team: Do you think these brands live their Purpose? Does it define why they exist?

Match the Logo Warm Up Activity Answers:

G. To challenge the status quo. To think differently.

C. To refresh the world and inspire moments of optimism and happiness.

B. To give people the power to build community so that we can bring the world closer together.

I. To empower every person and organization on the planet to achieve more.

E. To fulfill dreams of personal, All-American freedom.

F. To organize the world's information and make it universally accessible and useful.

D. To create happiness for people of all ages, everywhere.

A. To accelerate the world's transition to sustainable energy.

H. To inspire and nurture the human spirit — one person and one cup at a time.

Next, lead an open discussion with the groups via the "Ripple Effect Roundtable" Warm Up activity (Worksheet located on page 194).

Ripple Effect Rountable Warm Up Activity Instructions:

Have an open discussion about the following questions:.

1. Why are we / our community / the world better because our company exists?

2. What impact do we want to have on our team/our community / the world?

3. How can we make a positive impact through how we treat each other, the work we do and services we produce, and the way we engage with our community?

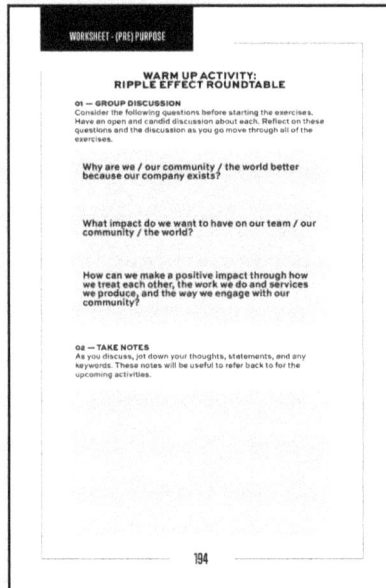

WORKSHEET - (PRE) PURPOSE

WARM UP ACTIVITY:
RIPPLE EFFECT ROUNDTABLE

01 — GROUP DISCUSSION
Consider the following questions before starting the exercises.
Have an open and candid discussion about each. Reflect on these
questions and the discussion as you go move through all of the
exercises.

Why are we / our community / the world better
because our company exists?

What impact do we want to have on our team / our
community / the world?

How can we make a positive impact through how
we treat each other, the work we do and services
we produce, and the way we engage with our
community?

02 — TAKE NOTES
As you discuss, jot down your thoughts, statements, and any
keywords. These notes will be useful to refer back to for the
upcoming activities.

194

If more clarity seems warranted after these warm-up activities, it could be beneficial to ask members if they have a personal Purpose, and for those comfortable, encourage them to share.

Run the Activities in the Workbook

Now that you've focused the group on Purpose, have your team go to the user activity section to complete the selected activity that will guide them in creating the company or team's Purpose.

Purpose Statement Examples

Need some help? Check out the examples below as well as the case studies at the end of this book. You can also find other templates available on **AlwaysLeadWithPurpose.com**. The examples below will be used in each section to help you see how PVTV can be crafted using hypothetical companies.

- SalesLive: *Our Purpose is to eliminate the tension between salespeople and their prospects.*
- GreenTech Solutions: *Our Purpose is to drive the global transition to sustainable energy.*

Post-Purpose Workshop

As the facilitator, you will need to ensure the dialogue remains rooted in the original vision for the Purpose statement. Don't let the broader team take it off track.

When concluding this team engagement, ensure all the voices feel as though they have been heard. Then, commit to a statement. It is unlikely you will reach a true consensus, yet everyone should understand why the decision was made and be ready to commit to this Purpose.

This process, steeped in your core Values, is a commitment to unity, aspiration, and differentiation.

—

Workshop: Envisioning Your Vision

Definition
Vision paints a picture of where your organization dreams to be in the next three to five years – it's all about your big goal and the roadmap you're crafting for the future.

Book Reference
In pages 125-130, Shera guides the team through crafting a Vision that is both aspirational and achievable. By envisioning a compelling future state, Shera's team sets a strategic path that aligns with their Purpose, ensuring that every action taken is intentional and directed toward a shared objective.

Here are questions she posed (and you should too!). Consider specific size, market reputation, or important attributes:
- Think about our company today . . . what are things you'd like us to improve or build upon?
- What kind of company do we ultimately aspire to become?
- What does success look like in three years along that journey? In five years?
- What would make you proud of our company and happy to have helped us accomplish?

Prep for the Meeting
- Familiarize yourself with key concepts and examples from the story.
- Prepare a brief presentation summarizing the significance of having a clear, compelling Vision.
- Develop open-ended questions to prompt reflection and discussion among team members about what they believe the organization's Vision might be.

Prep for the Selected Activity

There are two exercise types to cover kinesthetic and visual learners. Depending on your audience, you can select one of or both activities.

Around the Water Cooler (Option A)

Have the teams envision what others ideally say about the team. Think about overhearing a conversation around the water cooler. What would they love to hear being said about us by leadership, customers, and other teams? What successes of the team would they be discussing? This step is meant to warm-up the group and get you thinking positively about the team's impact.

What You'll Need

- Flipchart or whiteboard
- Markers and pens/pencils
- Post-it notes
- Downloaded worksheets from this playbook

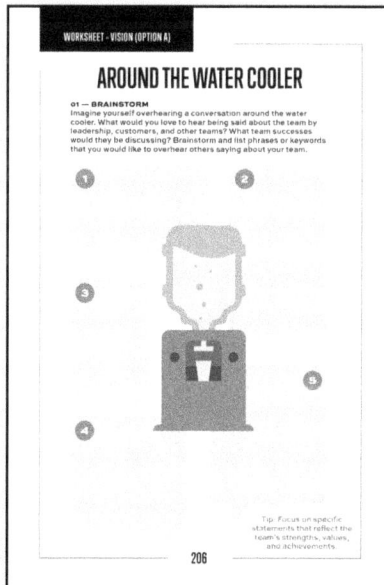

173

Vision Collage (Option B)

Explain to the team how we are going to create Vision collages to represent our desired future. Think about where we want to be in terms of financials, performance, customer feedback, and our standing in years one, three, and five. These collages will help us visualize success and guide us in crafting our Vision statements. Encourage creativity and personal expression while maintaining relevance to the team's goals and industry. And, remember: you may not achieve consensus, yet you do want to ensure everyone feels heard and understands why the final Vision statement was selected.

What You'll Need

- Computers or tablets with internet access and collage-making software (e.g., Canva, Adobe Spark)
- Projector or large screen for presentation
- Downloaded worksheets from this playbook

WORKSHEET - VISION (OPTION B)

VISION COLLAGE

YEAR ONE   YEAR THREE

YEAR FIVE

QUOTES

FINANCIAL   CUSTOMERS   TEAM

210

Kicking off the Vision Workshop

Creating Vision Statements can be a transformative process for a team, guiding them toward a shared future. Vision can be defined in many ways. To level set on what Vision is with the group so everyone uses the same definition, see the Glossary on 248. Review the exercise groups before the workshop and decide which one you want to do with your team.

Run the Activities in the Workbook

Depending on your audience, you can select one of the two exercises or do both together. We've developed two types of exercises for each section to cover both read/write and visual learners. By hosting the workshop and going through either or both exercises in each section, we capture the auditory and kinesthetic learners as well.

Vision Statement Examples

Below are example Vision Statements using the same hypothetical companies in the Purpose section:

- SalesLive: *Our Vision is to be the ultimate tool for our customers to achieve their sales goals.*
- GreenTech Solutions: *Our Vision is to become the leading provider of innovative, eco-friendly energy solutions by 2030.*

—

Workshop: Developing Your Tenets

Definition

Tenets are well-thought-out moves you work on to secure that major victory aligned with your Vision. If we were diving into business jargon, you might call them "Strategies" or "Approaches."

Book Reference

In *The Purpose Playbook* the exploration and establishment of Tenets are discussed in detail on pages 130-138. On these pages, Shera leads her team through a reflective process to identify the core principles that would govern their behavior and decision-making. This section of the book offers insights into how to articulate Tenets that are both aspirational and actionable, setting a standard for how the team operates both internally and in the broader marketplace. The book highlights the crucial role of Tenets in bridging the gap between the lofty ambitions of a Vision and the practical steps needed to achieve it, ensuring that the team's actions consistently align with its Purpose and Vision.

Prep for the Meeting

Review how Tenets are defined and prepare group discussion points. As previously noted, level setting the definition before exercises ensures everyone is on the same page upfront.

Prep for the Selected Activity

There are two exercise types to cover kinesthetic and visual learners. Depending on your audience, you can select one of or both activities.

Kitchen Sink Activity (Option A)

If you choose this activity, plan to give the team a full hour to run through all the work they need to achieve their Vision. Every thought counts and can help with building the themes needed to create your Tenets.

What You'll Need

- Post-it notes
- Markers
- Large workspace or boards for sorting
- Downloaded worksheets from this playbook

- Have the group list out everything they think they need to do to achieve their Vision. Remind them that every idea is a good one!
- Once ready, you'll organize the actions they uncover into groups and create themes. Have the team take the themes and prioritize them, and create Tenets from the themes and tweak them together. The group should have three to five Tenets total. If there are too many, combine statements that fall in the same category into one.
- If necessary, have the group vote on which statements should be their Tenets.

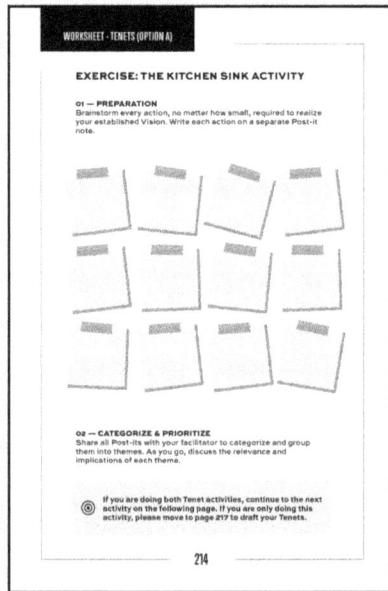

WORKSHEET · TENETS (OPTION A)

EXERCISE: THE KITCHEN SINK ACTIVITY

01 — PREPARATION
Brainstorm every action, no matter how small, required to realize your established Vision. Write each action on a separate Post-it note.

02 — CATEGORIZE & PRIORITIZE
Share all Post-its with your facilitator to categorize and group them into themes. As you go, discuss the relevance and implications of each theme.

If you are doing both Tenet activities, continue to the next activity on the following page. If you are only doing this activity, please move to page 217 to draft your Tenets.

214

From Challenges to Hope (Option B)

Using the word "fail" can be sensitive to some members. Make sure to be clear here that discussing their concerns as a team can prevent the failure from occurring (vulnerability-based trust is important here). The activity works best when you divide the team into small groups. Depending on the type of folks in your workshop, you may want to consider doing both activities in this section.

What You'll Need

- Flipchart or whiteboard
- Markers and pens/pencils
- Post-it notes
- Downloaded worksheets from this playbook

WORKSHEET - TENETS (OPTION 8)

FAILURES TO
HOPE STATEMENTS

01 — IDENTIFY POTENTIAL FAILURES
Write down five potential reasons the team might fail to achieve its
Vision, focusing on aspects within the team's control. Examples
might include a lack of communication or inadequate resource
allocation.

Failure Statements

02 — TRANSFROM CHALLENGES TO HOPE
Take the failures and rewrite them as positive "Hope Statements,"
or mitigation plans. For example, "Rapid tech changes could
outpace our product development cycles" could flip to "Establish
an innovation team that stays current on all emerging technologies
so that we can anticipate changes and adapt proactively."

Hope Statements

216

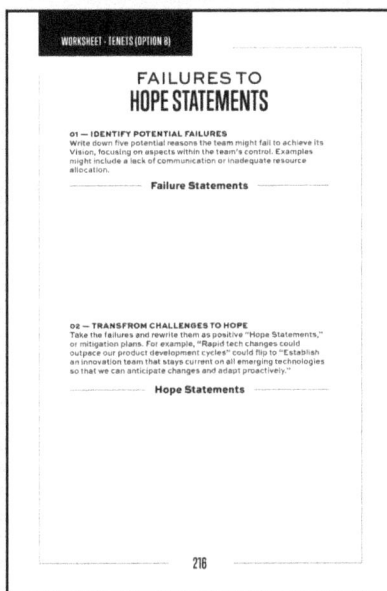

Tenet Examples

Below are example Tenets using the same hypothetical companies:

- SalesLive: *We will do this by. . .*
  - *Putting the customer first.*
  - *Believing in each other.*
  - *Focusing on profitable growth.*

- GreenTech Solutions: *We will do this by. . .*
  - *Innovating Continuously by Investing in R&D to create cutting-edge sustainable technologies.*
  - *Creating Strategic Partnerships by collaborating with governments, businesses, and communities to expand our impact.*
  - *Promoting the benefits of renewable energy to drive widespread adoption.*

Post-Tenets Bonus Activity

If you are a seasoned facilitator and want to take your team through a Flywheel activity, read on!

To ensure the Tenets effectiveness and direct contribution to realizing the Vision outlined in this playbook, consider the following approach.

The Flywheel Effect (Bonus Activity)

Validation through Direct Alignment: This is a quick task that confirms each Tenet, when put into practice, aligns directly with and contributes to the attainment of your Vision. Map each Tenet to specific aspects or objectives of the Vision, ensuring a clear and direct linkage.

Amplification through the Flywheel Effect: Consider pressure testing your Tenets' effectiveness by leveraging the Flywheel Effect (see Glossary for the definition on page 248), where each Tenet inherently supports and enhances the next, creating a virtuous cycle of continuous improvement and acceleration.

Much like an actual flywheel that goes faster as more is injected into each rotation, this approach ensures that the implementation of one Tenet naturally strengthens and sets the stage for the next, with each cycle drawing your Vision ever closer—similar to a beacon of light at the end of a tunnel that grows brighter with each pass. By viewing the Tenets through the lens of the Flywheel Effect, you create an interlinked approach to achieving your Vision.

Post-Flywheel Tenet Examples

Below are examples of using the flywheel effect with the same hypothetical companies:

Example 1: SalesLive

Vision: *Our Vision is to be the ultimate tool for our customers to achieve their sales goals.*

Tenets: *We will do this by. . .*
- *Putting the customer first.*
- *Believing in each other.*
- *Focusing on profitable growth.*

Flywheel Effect:
- *Customer-centric innovation leads to better products (putting the customer first).*
- *Trust and collaboration enhance product innovation (we believe in each other).*
- *Market expansion and awareness drive growth through effective strategies (profitable growth).*
- *Increased market presence builds a positive reputation and attracts more customers.*
- *Customer feedback and resources from the expanded customer base further fuel customer-centric innovation.*

The Flywheel Effect for SalesLive illustrates how focusing on customer-centric innovation, building trust and collaboration, expanding market reach, and engaging with the community all work together to create a virtuous cycle of continuous improvement. Each action supports and enhances the next, driving SalesLive toward its Vision of being the ultimate tool for customers to achieve their sales goals and fulfilling its Purpose of eliminating the tension between salespeople and their prospects.

Example 2: GreenTech Solutions:

Vision: *Our Vision is to become the leading provider of innovative, eco-friendly energy solutions by 2030.*

Tenets: *We will do this by. . .*
- *Innovating Continuously by Investing in R&D to create cutting-edge sustainable technologies.*
- *Creating Strategic Partnerships by collaborating with governments, businesses, and communities to expand our impact.*
- *Promoting the benefits of renewable energy to drive widespread adoption.*

Flywheel Effect:
- *Continuously innovating ensures GreenTech Solutions remains at the forefront of sustainable technology, creating products that attract attention and investment.*
- *Strategic partnerships leverage these innovations by forming strong alliances, expanding market reach and resource availability.*
- *Education and advocacy build market awareness and acceptance, driving demand for innovative products and partnerships.*
- *Increased market demand fuels further investment in R&D, enhancing GreenTech Solutions' ability to innovate continuously.*

Kicking off the Tenets Workshop

Review the glossary to describe to the group what Tenets are and why they are important. Make sure they know there are no wrong answers in these exercises. They should be considering everything that needs to occur to meet their Vision. Prep them to plan on spending a lot of time finding the themes out of all the work they've added.

Run the Activities in the Workbook

Depending on your audience, you can select one of the two activities or do both together. Before you decide which activity you want to do, here is Megan's insight from running a workshop that did these exercises simultaneously (side note: the co-author of this book, not the character, although Megan Scott was partially written after interviewing Megan Barney):

"I split the room up and let the group decide what exercise they wanted to do. There was a surprising balance between both and I credit that to having a balanced group of both strategic and tactical minds in the room. After they created their lists, we came back together to find themes and then draft the Tenets."

—

Workshop: Cultivating the Values

Definition

Values are soul-deep beliefs and top priorities that guide how someone or a group behaves. Imagine them as an inner compass of principles steering both personal and organizational choices.

Book Reference

The discussion on Values within *The Purpose Playbook* unfolds on pages 110-115, where Shera and her team delve into the foundational beliefs that reflect their core identity and ethos. The narrative describes a process of introspection and dialogue aimed at uncovering the Values that are truly central to the team's culture and Purpose. This passage underscores the significance of Values in guiding the team's interactions, behaviors, and choices, ensuring that their work achieves external success and fosters a positive and meaningful internal environment. By defining their Values, Shera's team commits to a set of shared convictions that strengthen their unity and integrity, emphasizing the importance of living these Values in their day-to-day operations and strategic decisions.

Prep for the Meeting

- Explain the importance of team Values in shaping a team's culture and behavior. Have the team spend a few minutes thinking through their top three to five personal Values; these can be work-related, ethical, or any aspect they believe is important for the team.
- Much like Tenets, Values need to be tested to ensure the team can live them day-to-day. We've added a third activity in this section to pressure test your team's Values after they're created.
- Recently, we've switched to start workshop discussions with an emphasis on Values. Diving deep into the team's

core principles has proven pivotal, bringing to light any underlying trust or conflict issues from the start. This focus has enhanced the effectiveness of our workshops, fostering a more cohesive and transparent team environment.

Prep for the Selected Activity

There are two exercise types to cover kinesthetic and visual learners. Depending on your audience, you can select one of or both activities.

Show Me Your Values (Option A)

What You'll Need

- Magazines, newspapers, or access to online resources
- Scissors, glue, and poster boards or digital collage tools
- Markers or pens
- A projector or large screen for presentations
- Downloaded worksheets from this playbook

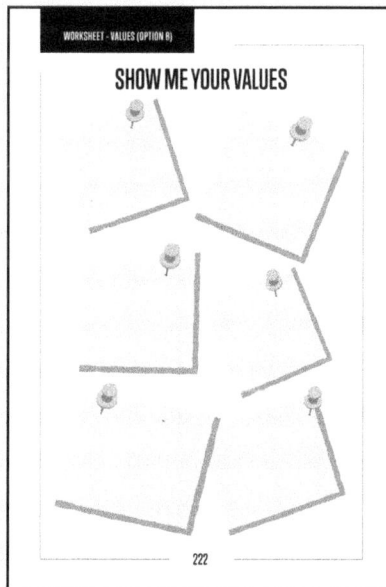

WORKSHEET - VALUES (OPTION B)

SHOW ME YOUR VALUES

222

185

Role Model Reflection (Option B)

What You'll Need

- Note cards or Post-it notes
- Pens or markers
- Flipchart or whiteboard
- Downloaded worksheets from this playbook

WORKSHEET - VALUES (OPTION B)

EXERCISE: MODELING

01 — IDENTIFY ROLE MODELS
List out people you want to emulate, what traits do they have and why do you want them? They can be someone personal to you, a celebrity, real person, or a character. Document the key values they have that you want your team to have too.

NAME   KEY TRAITS

02 — DISCUSS AND IDENTIFY THEMES
Together, analyze the identified Values and group similar themes. Decide what Value best represents all the words within the grouping, with the objective of reducing the number of Values into a draft of three to five.

- ♥ _____
- ♥ _____
- ♥ _____
- ♥ _____
- ♥ _____

03 — VOTE
Conclude by voting on the five core Values that best represent the team's ethos. We suggest the "2 Up 2 Down" voting system. The Values that move up the highest become the top 5 Values for your team. For more details on voting, see the last exercise.

224

Values Examples

Below are example Values using the same hypothetical companies:

- SalesLive: *We believe in* . .
  - *All for one and one for all.*
  - *Gaining advantage.*
  - *Always being two steps ahead.*

- GreenTech Solutions *We believe in* . .

186

- *Sustainability: Eco-friendly practices in all we do.*
- *Integrity: Transparency and honesty always.*
- *Innovation: Constantly developing new solutions.*
- *Community: Uplifting the communities we serve.*

Post-Values Activity

After your team has completed the first activity, review each identified Value to collectively define what it means in the context of the team's work and interactions (We will guide you through this in the next activity!)

It is critical to ensure everyone defines the Value the same; a word can be meaningful and defined differently from person-to-person, so make sure to discuss the definition of the word in addition to what the word means to your team. Make sure to document the definition so you can use it in your detailed PVTV document as described in the "Putting it All Together" section.

Value-to-Behavior Mapping (Post-Values Activity)

After identifying and defining the Values that are most meaningful, this activity creates alignment with everyday work activities to foster a deeper understanding and practical application of these Values.

What You'll Need

- Note cards or Post-it notes
- Pens or markers
- Large whiteboard to create the grid

Kicking off the Values Workshop

Level set the group by having one or two team members discuss a person they would want to emulate with the group. They can be someone personal to them, a celebrity, real, or a character. The activities will lead you through creating and grouping the categories of the Values provided.

Run the Activities in the Workbook

Depending on your audience, you can select one of the first two exercises, or do both together. Regardless of which activities you select, *please complete the post-Values activity afterward* to pressure test the Values the team created.

—

Workshop: Putting it All Together

Congratulations! You have just completed facilitating your team to collectively shape and finalize their Purpose, Vision, Tenets, & Values. In this final step of documenting the PVTV, the team should be intentional in describing each statement. Once drafted, the expanded version should deepen your team's understanding, ensuring these foundational pillars truly resonate within every facet of your organization. Have the team memorize the core PVTV statement, but they can use the expanded version when additional explanation is helpful (for instance, when a new employee joins the team).

PVTV Expansion
What You'll Need   • Notes from prior workshop sessions   • Downloaded worksheets from this playbook

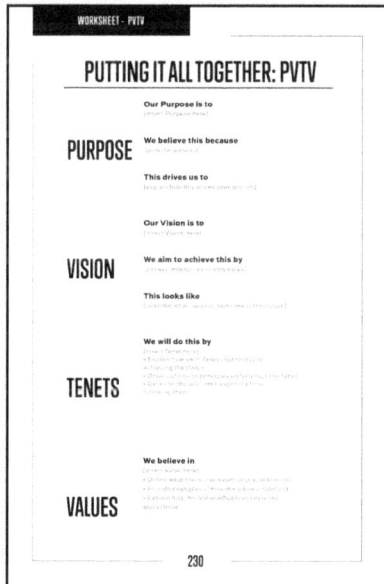

Kicking off the Final Workshop

Lead your group through each area and explain how to expand each item. Follow the template below to guide your team through this final piece of the PVTV. We've provided a template you can use within the activity section.

Purpose Expansion: Have the team discuss why they believe in the Purpose and document the reasons. Discuss how the Purpose will drive the team's actions. This statement is the lifeblood of the organization, making the abstract tangible and impactful.

Articulate Your Vision: To expand your Vision, list out the key milestones and strategies that are necessary to be successful. Describe what success looks like for each item in your list.

Tenets in Action: As the key strategies or pillars that will enable you to achieve your Vision and fulfill your Purpose, explain how each Tenet contributes to achieving the Vision. Detail actions or principles underlying each Tenet. Describe the outcomes expected from following them.

Values in Volume: Choosing Values to influence decisions and actions ensures the team understands how to work better together. Make sure each Value is defined in practical terms. This is a good time to take out the notes you saved from your Values workshop!

ACTIVITIES

CRAFTING PVTV
(FOR WORKSHOP PARTICIPANTS)

Welcome to the fun part – it's time to craft your PVTV!

Before you dive in, please remember these activities are designed to be interactive and thought-provoking: fostering open dialogue, reflection, and collaboration crucial for shaping your team's Purpose, Vision, Tenets, & Values (PVTV).

Here is what to expect:

P—Identifying Your Purpose
V—Envisioning Your Vision
T—Developing Your Tenets
V—Cultivating the Values
PVTV—Putting it All Together

P VTV

Identifying Your Purpose

Purpose is the core reason your organization exists, beyond making money. It's the driving force that guides your actions and decisions, and helps you define your path. It answers the question, "Why do we get up in the morning?"

On pages 116-123, Shera's team embarks on a journey to define their Purpose. This section illustrates the importance of Purpose in providing direction and motivation for the team, driving them to align their actions with their deeper 'why.' By identifying their Purpose, Shera's team sets a clear foundation that informs their decisions and inspires their daily efforts, ensuring they remain focused on their ultimate goal and objectives and the impact they wish to achieve.

Suggested Activities

There are two warm up activities (Match the Logo and Ripple Effect Roundtable), followed by two exploration activities (Uncover the Core and Crafting the Future through Dream Headlines) to help generate your first Purpose statement. For the exploration there are two options to choose from (your facilitator may have already decided which one your group will complete). If you finish with one exercise and feel you could benefit from more to the core of your statement, we recommend you do both activities.

WARM-UP ACTIVITY: MATCH THE LOGOS

Match the logos to the Purpose statements:

_____   _____   _____

_____   _____   _____

_____   _____   _____

A. To accelerate the world's transition to sustainable energy.

B. To give people the power to build community so that we can bring the world closer together.

C. To refresh the world and inspire moments of optimism and happiness.

D. To create happiness for people of all ages, everywhere.

E. To fulfill dreams of personal, All-American freedom.

F. To organize the world's information and make it universally accessible and useful.

G. To challenge the status quo. To think differently.

H. To inspire and nurture the human spirit — one person and one cup at a time.

I. To empower every person and organization on the planet to achieve more.

WARM UP ACTIVITY:
RIPPLE EFFECT ROUNDTABLE

01 — GROUP DISCUSSION
Consider the following questions before starting the exercises. Have an open and candid discussion about each. Reflect on these questions and the discussion as you go move through all of the exercises.

Why are we / our community / the world better because our company exists?

What impact do we want to have on our team / our community / the world?

How can we make a positive impact through how we treat each other, the work we do and services we produce, and the way we engage with our community?

02 — TAKE NOTES
As you discuss, jot down your thoughts, statements, and any keywords. These notes will be useful to refer back to for the upcoming activities.

Purpose Activity Option A:
Uncover the Core

Objective:
This exercise is designed to delve deep into the heart of why your team exists, peeling back the layers through persistent inquiry. The objective is to arrive at the fundamental Purpose that drives every action and decision within your team.

Duration:
60 - 90 minutes

Expected Outcome
A collaboratively-crafted Purpose statement that authentically represents the foundational reason behind its existence, ensuring every team member is aligned with and committed to this central guiding principle.

ACTIVITY: UNCOVER THE CORE

01 — BRAINWRITING
Creating Why Statements

1. Everyone on the team has a blank index card at the start.

2. Using the notes you took from the group discussion, write your suggestion for the team's Purpose statement on the top line(s) of your index card.)

3. Pass your card to the person next to you. The next person should answer "why" to the statement you wrote on your card, writing it down. (You will answer the card passed to you.)

4. Continue passing the cards around the room until several statements are on each card. Keep going until each card is full or you run out of answers.

02 — GROUP DISCUSSION
When your team is ready, have a volunteer share the statements on the index cards with the rest of the group.

1. Discuss any themes and make those themes visible to the team for the next part of the activity.

2. As a group, examine the various Purpose statements.

3. Discuss recurring keywords, themes, and insights that emerge from these collective reflections. Take note of them on the next page.

4. Start to draft your final Purpose Statements using the space provided on the next page.

CHECKPOINT: This final statement should:
- begin with "Our Purpose is ... "
- be short and powerful,
- be unattainable (or close to it),
- and it should distinguish the company or team from competitors or other teams.

KEYWORDS TO
PURPOSE STATEMENTS

Drop keywords here to later
shape them into statements.

Keywords & Thoughts

Purpose Statements

Purpose Activity Option B: Crafting the Future through Dream Headlines

Objective:
This exercise is designed to propel the team into the future. Driven by their collective Purpose, it allows members to visualize and articulate what they ultimately want to achieve.

By imagining these future successes, the team can more clearly define what they aspire to accomplish and the core Purpose that will guide them toward these goals.

Duration:
45 - 60 minutes

Expected Outcome
A forward-looking, aspirational Purpose statement rooted in the collective dreams and futures of its members. This statement will serve as a guide, focusing your team's efforts and decisions on achieving the significant successes they imagine.

ACTIVITY: CRAFTING THE FUTURE THROUGH DREAM HEADLINES

01 — CRAFT YOUR FUTURE

Envision your team's future, considering the significant successes you would achieve. Think broadly and ambitiously, reflecting on your desired impact and outcomes. Reflect on why you exist, how you make a difference, and your collective strengths and how those contribute to your future success.

Based on this reflection, write a newspaper-style headline that captures the essence of this future success. Include accompanying content that describes the achievement in more detail — imagining it as a story covered by a major publication. Encourage creativity and depth, allowing for imagery and narratives that truly resonate with the team's aspirations.

Below is an example press release. Use the template on the next page to bring your press release to life.

SALESLIVE

PRESS RELEASE

SalesLive's Purpose-Driven Innovation Transforms Digital Sales Landscape

Date Release: 07/02/2027

New York, NY - SalesLive has redefined the digital sales landscape by staying true to their purpose of eliminating the tension between salespeople and their prospects. Through innovative, customer-centric solutions and pioneering technology, Sales Live has achieved remarkable success, reporting a 45% increase in revenue this past fiscal year. Led by CEO Shera Jones , the company's visionary leadership, strategic partnerships, and commitment to sustainability have propelled it to the forefront of the industry, empowering businesses to thrive in the digital era.

PRESS RELEASE

FROM DREAMS
TO REALITY

01 — PRESENT YOUR PRESS RELEASE

Select a presenter to represent your group and have this person present their headlines and stories to the room.

Allow each presenter time to share the story and the vision behind their headline.

02 — FIND THE THEMES

After all presentations, identify common themes, keywords, and visions that emerge from the dream headlines.

What are the recurring elements that seem to define the team's envisioned success?

Add them to the section on the next page.

03— BUILD YOUR PURPOSE STATEMENT

1. Using the identified themes and keywords, craft proposed Purpose statements. We've given you a scratchpad on the next page.

2. Once several Purpose statements have been created and reviewed with the group, vote on each statement. Continue refining and voting until the team reaches a consensus on one final Purpose statement that accurately represents your shared aspirations.

Tip: Consensus tends to be a lofty goal. Instead, make sure all voices feel heard and considered and then move to commit.

CHECKPOINT: This final statement should:
- begin with "Our Purpose is . . . "
- be short and powerful,
- be unattainable (or close to it),
- and it should distinguish the company or team from competitors or other teams.

THEMES TO
PURPOSE STATEMENTS

Themes & Values

Purpose Statements

P V TV
Envisioning Your Vision

Vision paints a picture of where your organization dreams to be in the next three to five years – it's all about your big goal and the roadmap you're crafting for the future.

In pages 125-130, Shera guides the team through crafting a Vision that is both aspirational and achievable. The Vision serves as a North Star, providing clear direction and inspiring the team to work toward its long-term goal. By envisioning a compelling future state, Shera's team sets a strategic path that aligns with their Purpose, ensuring that every action taken is intentional and directed towards a shared objective.

Suggested Activities

Read the next pages to have group discussions and complete the activities to generate your first Vision statement. There are two exercises to choose from, if you have a facilitator they have probably already decided which one your group will complete. If you finish with one exercise and feel you need more to get to the core of your statement, we recommend you do both activities in each section.

WARM UP ACTIVITY: VISION PREPARATION

01 — GROUP DISCUSSION

Consider the following questions before starting the exercises. Have an open and candid discussion about each. Reflect on these questions and the discussion as you go move through all of the exercises.

Think about our company today . . . what are things you'd like us to improve or build upon?

What kind of company do we ultimately aspire to become?

What would make you proud of our company and happy to have helped us accomplish? (e.g., specific size, market reputation, or important attributes)

What does success look like in three years along that journey? In five years?

02 — TAKE NOTES

As you discuss, jot down your thoughts, statements, and any keywords. These notes will be useful to refer back to for the upcoming activities.

THE PURPOSE PLAYBOOK: ACTIVITIES

Vision Activity Option A:
Around the Water Cooler

Objective:

To uncover and define the team's Vision by imagining what others would say about the team, mimicking casual but insightful conversations that might occur around a typical office water cooler.

Duration:

45 - 60 minutes

Expected Outcome

A clear and unified Vision statement reflecting the team's strengths and Values. This Vision now guides and motivates the team, enhancing cohesion and alignment.

AROUND THE WATER COOLER

01 — BRAINSTORM

Imagine yourself overhearing a conversation around the water cooler. What would you love to hear being said about the team by leadership, customers, and other teams? What team successes would they be discussing? Brainstorm and list phrases or keywords that you would like to overhear others saying about your team.

1

2

3

5

4

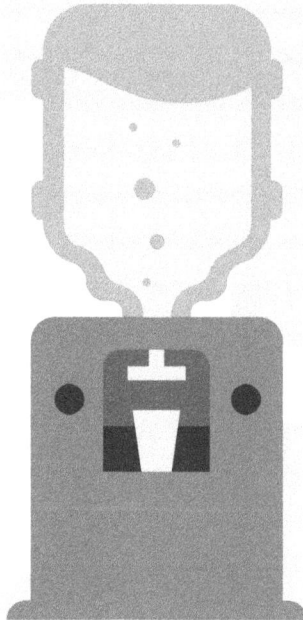

Tip: Focus on specific statements that reflect the team's strengths, values, and achievements.

02 — SHARE & ORGANIZE

Have each representative from your group present the brainstormed phrases and keywords. You or the facilitator can write these down on a flipchart or whiteboard for everyone to see. Once all ideas are presented, identify common themes by grouping similar or related items together.

03 — CRAFT THE VISION STATEMENT

Using the themes, begin crafting a Vision statement that encapsulates the positive attributes and achievements listed.

This Vision should be aspirational yet achievable, reflecting the essence of what makes the team unique and successful

OUR VISION IS TO BE

adjective

FOR   THAT WILL

noun   outcome or impact

outcome or impact (cont'd)

04 — DISCUSS AND VOTE

Once several Vision statements have been created and reviewed with the group, vote on each statement. Continue refining and voting until the team reaches a consensus on one final Vision statement that accurately represents your shared aspirations.

👁 _____

👁 _____

👁 _____

🏵 _____

CHECKPOINT: This final statement should:
- begin with "Our Vision is to . . "
- not conflict with the Purpose
- get closer to achieving the Purpose
- be ambitious, yet feasible

Vision Activity Option B: Vision Collage

Objective:
To visually express the team's future aspirations and concrete objectives using a collage, facilitating a deeper understanding and commitment to the shared Vision.

Duration:
60 - 120 minutes

Expected Outcome
The team will create a unified Vision statement that incorporates key success indicators and reflects shared aspirations. This Vision will guide future efforts, ensuring alignment and cohesion among team members.

ACTIVITY: FIND INSPIRATION WITH A VISION COLLAGE

01 — PREPARATION

Write your thoughts on key indicators of success for the team. For example: financials, performance metrics, or customer satisfaction. Include the team's position at future milestones (one, three, and five years). Think broadly yet ensure these are achievable and relevant indicators.

Key Indicators of Success

02 — CREATE YOUR COLLAGE

Use images, quotes, graphs, and any other visuals that represent your view of the team's future success based on the key indicators listed. If you are doing this on your computer, feel free to use online tools. If you want to create one with magazines or text, use the provided template on the next page.

03 — PRESENT AND DISCUSS

Present your Vision collage to the group (or select a representative if you are completing this task as a group), explaining the significance of the chosen images and how they relate to the team's key success indicators. After each presentation, you will want to allow a brief Q&A session for clarification and discussion.

VISION COLLAGE

YEAR ONE   **YEAR THREE**

                               YEAR FIVE

QUOTES

FINANCIAL   **CUSTOMERS**   **TEAM**

04 — IDENTIFY COMMON THEMES

As a group, discuss the themes and patterns you see across the different collages. You or the facilitator can write these themes on a flipchart or whiteboard. This step helps consolidate each perspective into collective insights.

05 — CRAFT THE VISION STATEMENT

Using the common themes as a foundation, work together to draft one to three Vision statements.

These statements should be aspirational, yet grounded in the reality of the team's objectives and the key indicators of success identified earlier.

OUR VISION IS TO BE

adjective

FOR   THAT WILL

noun   outcome or impact

outcome or impact (cont'd)

06 — DISCUSS AND VOTE

Discuss the merits and potential challenges of each draft Vision statement. Based on group feedback, refine the wording and focus of each statement. Once the group feels satisfied with the final drafts, conduct a vote using stickers or markers to choose the statement that best aligns with the team's shared aspirations.

CHECKPOINT: This final statement should:
- begin with "Our Vision is to . . "
- not conflict with the Purpose
- get closer to achieving the Purpose
- be ambitious, yet feasible

211

PV**T**V
Developing Your Tenets

Tenets, when well-thought-out, drive you to secure that major victory aligned with your Vision. Diving into business jargon, you might call them "Strategy Statements" or "Approaches."

The exploration and establishment of Tenets are discussed in detail on pages 130-136. On these pages, Shera leads her team through a reflective process to identify the core principles that would govern their behavior and decision-making. This section of the book offers insights into how to articulate Tenets that are both aspirational and actionable, setting a standard for how the team operates both internally and in the broader marketplace. The book highlights the crucial role of Tenets in bridging the gap between the lofty ambitions of a Vision and the practical steps needed to achieve it, ensuring that the team's actions consistently align with its Purpose and Vision.

Suggested Activities

Follow the pages to have group discussions and complete the activities to generate your Tenets. There are two exercises in this section that are better together than apart. If you still choose to do only one, look for the prompts to guide you to the right pages.

Tenets Activity Option A:
The Kitchen Sink Activity

Objective:

To identify all necessary actions to achieve the Vision and develop Tenets that encapsulate these efforts.

Duration:

45 - 60 minutes

Expected Outcome

Upon completing these workshop activities, you will have crafted three to five key Tenets that are memorable and can seamlessly integrate into every discussion.

EXERCISE: THE KITCHEN SINK ACTIVITY

01 — PREPARATION

Brainstorm every action, no matter how small, required to realize your established Vision. Write each action on a separate Post-it note.

02 — CATEGORIZE & PRIORITIZE

Share all Post-its with your facilitator to categorize and group them into themes. As you go, discuss the relevance and implications of each theme.

If you are doing both Tenet activities, continue to the next activity on the following page. If you are only doing this activity, please move to page 217 to draft your Tenets.

Tenets Activity Option B:
Why We Failed

Objective:

To transform potential setbacks into motivating Tenets that guide the team toward achieving their Vision.

Duration:

45 - 60 minutes

Expected Outcome

Three to five key Tenets that are memorable and can seamlessly integrate into every discussion.

.

FAILURES TO
HOPE STATEMENTS

01 — IDENTIFY POTENTIAL FAILURES

Write down five potential reasons the team might fail to achieve its Vision, focusing on aspects within the team's control. Examples might include a lack of communication or inadequate resource allocation.

—————— Failure Statements ——————

02 — TRANSFROM CHALLENGES TO HOPE

Take the failures and rewrite them as positive "Hope Statements," or mitigation plans. For example, "Rapid tech changes could outpace our product development cycles" could flip to "Establish an innovation team that stays current on all emerging technologies so that we can anticipate changes and adapt proactively."

—————— Hope Statements ——————

216

EXERCISE: WHY WE FAILED

03 — DISCUSS AND CATEGORIZE

Each group shares both its failures and hopes with the room so that themes can be identified from the hope statements. Have a brief discussion on each theme and consider, if successful, the impact it would make on getting closer to your Vision.

Once you have prioritized the themes with the greatest impact, draft your Tenets using the activity instructions below and the space provided on the next page.

◎ **If you are skipping the Why We Failed activity, please start here.**

If you chose to do both The Kitchen Sink and Why We Failed activity, make sure to bring in the themes from both activities to help draft your Tenet Statements.

DRAFT YOUR TENETS

Based on the identified themes, work with your group to formulate Tenet statements (using the template on the next page).

These should encapsulate the actions and principles that will drive the team towards its Vision. Ensure these Tenets are actionable and aligned with the team's objectives.

Share your drafted Tenets with the larger group. Evaluate each based on its alignment with the Vision and its measurability. Debate their merits and refine them as necessary.

Once refined, conduct a group vote to select the top three to five Tenets. Commit to upholding these Tenets as guiding principles moving forward.

WE WILL DO THIS BY...

TENET ONE

TENET TWO

TENET THREE

TENET FOUR

TENET FIVE

CHECKPOINT: This final statements should:
- begin with "We will do this by .. "
- point in the direction to achieve the Vision
- be measurable statements that can be regularly evaluated
- focus the team on what must be accomplished

PVT**V**

Cultivating the Values

Values are soul-deep beliefs and top priorities that guide how someone or a group behaves. Imagine them as an inner compass of principles steering both personal and organizational choices.

The discussion on Values unfolds on pages 110-115, where Shera and her team delve into the foundational beliefs that reflect their core identity and ethos. The narrative describes a process of introspection and dialogue aimed at uncovering the Values that are truly central to the team's culture and Purpose. This passage underscores the significance of Values in guiding the team's interactions, behaviors, and choices, ensuring that their work achieves external success and fosters a positive and meaningful internal environment. By defining their Values, Shera's team commits to a set of shared convictions that strengthen their unity and integrity, emphasizing the importance of living these Values in their day-to-day operations and strategic decisions.

Suggested Activities

Read the next pages to have group discussions and complete the activities to generate your Values. There are two exercises to choose from; if you have a facilitator they have likely already decided which one your group will complete.

Values Activity Option A:
Show Me Your Values

Objective:

To visually express and share what team members consider crucial Values, facilitating a deeper understanding and consensus.

Duration:

45 - 60 minutes

Expected Outcome

The Values you define will provide a solid foundation for your team, guiding their actions and ensuring consistency with their Purpose and Vision.

.

ACTIVITY: SHOW ME YOUR VALUES

01 — PREPARATION
Individually or in small groups, using magazines or the Internet, search for and select images, quotes, or symbols that represent a perceived core team or company Value.

Using the template on the next page, assemble these into a collage that visually expresses these Value.

02 — PRESENTATION AND STORYTELLING
Each individual or group presents their collage, sharing stories or scenarios from work that exemplify the depicted Values. Encourage detailed narratives to provide context and deepen understanding.

Quality

Trust

03 — ANALYSIS AND CONSENSUS
After all presentations, collaboratively identify overlapping themes and note any gaps. Discuss the consistency and diversity of the expressed Values, and how they align with the team's Vision and Purpose.

Loyalty

04 — REFLECTION
Reflect on the proposed Values by discussing:
- The shared meaning of each Value within the team.
- Specific actions and behaviors that demonstrate each Value.
- Potential misinterpretations or negative impacts.
- Strategies for measuring and maintaining these Values.

05 — VOTE
Conclude by voting on the five core Values that best represent the team's ethos. We suggest the "2 Up 2 Down" voting system. It is a method where every person evaluates all options and chooses 2 of their most favorite and 2 of their least favorite choices. We recommend having all values viewable on a wall or screen, each person goes to the wall and moves two Values up and two Values down. The Values that move up the highest become the top Values for your team.

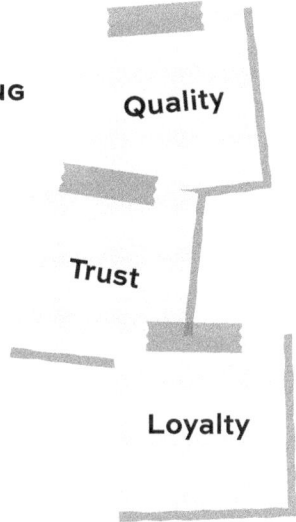

SHOW ME YOUR VALUES

Value Activity Option B: Role Model Reflection

Objective:

To identify core Values by reflecting on traits admired in others and determining how these can integrate into the team's ethos.

Duration:

45 - 60 minutes

Expected Outcome

A solid foundation for your team, guiding their actions and ensuring consistency with their Purpose and Vision.

.

EXERCISE: MODELING

01 — IDENTIFY ROLE MODELS

List out people you want to emulate, what traits do they have and why do you want them? They can be someone personal to you, a celebrity, real person, or a character. Document the key Values they have that you want your team to have too.

NAME   **KEY TRAITS**

02 — DISCUSS AND IDENTIFY THEMES

Together, analyze the identified Values and group similar themes. Decide what Value best represents all the words within the grouping, with the objective of reducing the number of Values into a draft of three to five.

03 — VOTE

Conclude by voting on the five core Values that best represent the team's ethos. We suggest the "2 Up 2 Down" voting system. The Values that move up the highest become the top 5 Values for your team. For more details on voting, see the last activity.

Post-Values Activity:
Value-to-Behavior Mapping

Objective:

Nice job! Your team has completed defining the Values that are most meaningful to them. Now let's make sure they align with their everyday work activities in order to foster a deeper understanding and practical application of these Values in daily operations.

Note: This exercise should not be skipped; this helps you pressure test the Values you created (resulting from activity A and/or B).

Duration:

90 minutes

Expected Outcome

A team clearly aligning their core Values with specific behaviors across various work situations, ensuring that the Values are unifying, non-negotiable, succinct, clear, and actionable/measurable — thus ready for full commitment.

VALUE TO
BEHAVIOR MAPPING

01 — PREPARATION
Create a simple table on a large board (we've provided a template on the next page, too).

List the core Values along the top and typical work activities (like team meetings, project planning) along the side.

Fill in each field with the expected behaviors when that Value is activated

02 — MAP VALUES TO BEHAVIORS
Fill in the matrix where you see a direct connection between a Value and an activity.

Briefly describe an example of how the Value influences behavior in that specific situation.

03— GROUP DISCUSSION
Once complete, each team member can elaborate on the examples they've posted, explaining how these behaviors align with the Values. This is also a time to address any inconsistencies or challenges in applying these Values.

CHECKPOINT: The final Values you select should:
- be unifying
- be non-negotiable
- be succinct and clear
- be actionable and measurable

VALUE MATRIX

INSTRUCTIONS:
- Add your team Values in top boxes
- Add team activities on the side
- Fill in each field with the expected behaviors when that Value is activated

Note: This graphic is representative only. Please use a larger space for mapping out and filling in your matrix, such as a posterboard or whiteboard.

Core Values

Activity

PVTV
Putting it All Together

Congratulations on reaching this pivotal moment! Your team has collectively shaped and finalized the Purpose, Vision, Tenets, & Values (PVTV) that will steer the course of your journey.

Suggested Activities

This final piece of documenting the expanded PVTV can be done at the leadership level. You'll want to be intentional with describing each statement to remove any misunderstanding across the team.

Once drafted, the expanded version should deepen your team's understanding and ensure these foundational pillars truly resonate within every facet of your organization.

PVTV Activity: PVTV Expansion

Purpose Expansion: Discuss why you believe in the Purpose and document the reasons. Discuss how the Purpose will drive your team's actions. This statement is the lifeblood of your organization, making the abstract tangibly impactful.

Articulate Your Vision: To expand your Vision, list out the key milestones and strategies that are necessary to be successful. Describe what success looks like for each item in your list.

Tenets in Action: As the key strategies or pillars that will enable you to achieve your Vision and fulfill your Purpose, explain how each Tenet contributes to achieving the Vision. Detail actions or principles underlying each Tenet. Describe the outcomes expected from following them.

Values in Volume: Leverage stories or accolades the team may observe of a colleague exemplifying a Value. This is a good time to take out the notes you saved from your Values workshop.

Once you're happy with your expanded PVTV, the next step is to share it with your whole team. Integrate it into daily routines, meetings, and decision-making processes. You'll want to embrace this part of the playbook for at least three to sixmonths before moving into operationalizing your PVTV.

PUTTING IT ALL TOGETHER: PVTV

PURPOSE

Our Purpose is to
[insert Purpose here]

We believe this because
[provide reasons]

This drives us to
[explain how this drives your actions]

VISION

Our Vision is to
[insert Vision here]

We aim to achieve this by
[list key milestones or strategies]

This looks like
[describe what success looks like in this future]

We will do this by

[insert Tenets here]

• Explain how each Tenet contributes to achieving the Vision.

• Detail actions or principles underlying each Tenet.

• Describe the outcomes expected from following them.

TENETS

We believe in

[insert Values here]

• Define what this Value means in practical terms.

• Provide examples of how this Value is lived out

• Explain how this Value influences decisions and actions.

VALUES

CASE STUDIES

LEARNING FROM OTHERS

Starting something new can often feel like you're staring at a blank sheet of paper, unsure where to begin. Some call this writer's block, yet it's not just about lacking ideas—it's about needing that initial spark. One of the best ways to overcome this is by looking at how other companies have tackled similar challenges.

The challenge for Jeff, Megan, and Teresa, though, is predicting what type of companies will read this book. Should the Playbook focus on large corporations or small businesses? Are we talking to well-established brands, creative agencies, or perhaps startups? After much discussion, it was decided the approach should attempt to be flexible enough to be relevant to any type of organization.

So, in the following pages, you will read how this works in practice from several perspectives: small, medium, and large. You'll learn how Jeff is injecting Purpose into a printing company and how Megan has successfully implemented the PVTV across multiple teams (within a large organization). Additionally, Teresa shares her journey of turning a budding solo venture into a fully-fledged business that can operate independently of her. As we continue to use this playbook and gather more stories from users, we'll share more examples on AlwaysLeadWithPurpose.com to enrich your understanding and application of the concepts discussed.

Case Study for Foundational Work: Building Team Trust

SalesLive

Before embarking on the PVTV process, laying a solid foundation for a highly functioning team is crucial. Shera, CEO of SalesLive, realized her team was not ready to support each other effectively, prompting her to work with Charles to assess and enhance their team dynamics. (Note: For more details on their initial assessment, please refer to **Chapter 1: Trusting Team**.) This case study illustrates how Shera and her team built the essential characteristics of team readiness, addressing strategic conviction, empowered change, purposeful integration, and unified commitment to ensure they were fully prepared for the PVTV journey. (Note: Readers should also review the **Assessing Readiness** list found in the Foundational Work section of the playbook for a comprehensive understanding of these characteristics.)

When Shera first assessed her leadership team's readiness for the PVTV process, she discovered significant gaps. Charles, a trusted advisor, helped facilitate this assessment, which revealed that while there were many positive aspects within the group, the team lacked the mutual trust and support necessary for a high-functioning unit. This realization prompted an effort to address these deficiencies and prepare the team for the transformative journey ahead.

After Charles completed his workshop with the team, Shera took another look at the Readiness List Charles left so she could be completely sure they were ready. The following are the further steps she took with her team.

To foster **strategic conviction**, the team emphasized shared results over individual accomplishments. They worked to understand and align with the company's Purpose, ensuring that every team member felt empowered to drive change. Regular "Trust Talks" were introduced, where members openly shared personal challenges and successes, building a foundation of trust. Shera's own admission of past delegation failures set the tone for vulnerability, encouraging others to share their experiences without fear of judgment.

To enhance **purposeful integration**, Shera moderated sessions that delved into team members' differing views on strategic initiatives. Through role-playing exercises, the team learned to appreciate diverse perspectives and motivations, such as Rachel's conservative budgeting aimed at sustainability rather than resistance to innovation. These sessions transformed potential conflicts into opportunities for deeper understanding and innovation, reinforcing the team's commitment to the company's Purpose.

The team also focused on **actions speaking louder than words** by ensuring everyone was ready to embody PVTV principles in daily operations and strategic decisions. They collaboratively developed detailed action plans for upcoming projects, clearly defining each member's responsibilities in alignment with their strengths and career goals. This clarity helped prevent vague commitments and misaligned expectations, leading to more realistic and enthusiastic engagement in their roles.

Establishing the **plumbing to support PVTV** involved creating an accountability framework where team members reported on their progress during weekly meetings, highlighting accomplishments and barriers. This open structure fostered a supportive environment, viewing challenges as collective issues rather than individual failures. Regular check-ins and feedback loops encouraged ongoing communication about successes and obstacles, deepening the team's accountability and support for one another.

Finally, **unified pulse and clear conviction** were achieved by setting ambitious performance targets aligned with the new marketing strategy. Each member's contributions were reviewed and agreed upon collectively, ensuring that individual efforts supported team and organizational objectives. Monthly review sessions were conducted to assess progress, discuss adjustments, and celebrate achievements, maintaining alignment and focus on a common goal.

In sum, through strategic conviction, purposeful integration, clear accountability, and unified commitment, Shera and her team at SalesLive successfully laid the foundation for a highly functioning team, fully prepared to embrace and implement the PVTV framework. For a more detailed understanding of the readiness process, please refer to the beginning of the book.

Case Studies for Activities: Crafting PVTV

Moving forward on your own without the continuous guidance of an expert can often feel like navigating without a map. Even after initial consultations, the challenge of applying what you've learned independently can be daunting.

If you choose to do this on your own, be sure to ponder questions like: How could your team have pushed your strategies further? In what ways might they have made our approaches more distinct? This self-analysis demonstrates your commitment to continual improvement and provides a transparent example to the rest of your team of how critical self-reflection is when it comes to fine-tuning your strategies and operations.

Gerald Printing & Liberty Imaging

In this case study, we explore how Jeff, who leads Purpose Group—a Purpose-Driven Holding Company—works with the leadership team to apply *The Purpose Playbook* methodology to transform the Gerald Printing & Liberty Imaging company's approach to Purpose. (Note: Purpose Group specializes in acquiring and reinvigorating small businesses, aiming to create more inspired and engaged employees.) This case study serves as an example for facilitators and their teams of small- to medium-sized companies, offering inspiration on how to effectively implement the principles of PVTV to bring client and team member Visions to life.

Purpose *Our Purpose is to bring visions to life.*

Bringing Client Visions to Life

We specialize in turning clients' rough ideas into polished, real-world products. Whether it's a sample, a sketch, or a vague notion, we have the experience and expertise to bring it to life. We thrive on making the abstract concrete, delivering results that surpass expectations.

Bringing Team Member Visions to Life

We embrace the diverse visions our team members hold for their careers and are committed to nurturing their growth accordingly. For those aiming to excel in their roles, we offer personalized training and support. And for those seeking leadership positions, we provide mentorship and clear paths to advancement. We believe in helping every team member reach their goals while contributing to our collective success.

Vision *Our Vision is to become the first choice for our clients and our teams*

We know we are not the only choice for our clients and teams. Still, we can be the FIRST choice by delivering exceptional value, quality, and innovative solutions across our various products. We're dedicated to making our company the preferred destination for our team members, offering growth opportunities and a supportive personal and professional development environment.

Success will be gauged through increased client satisfaction, repeat business, and brand recognition, as well as enhanced employee engagement and retention, built on a vibrant company culture of teamwork and creativity. Our commitment is to foster lasting relationships, sustainable growth, and positive community impact.

Tenets *We will do this by ...*

Developing a strong and fulfilled team

We cannot fulfill our Vision without our team of dedicated professionals. We will build a strong and fulfilled team by having a diverse and inclusive workplace. We believe that a variety of backgrounds increases our creativity and innovation, and makes us adaptable to a changing marketplace. We will cultivate a positive culture, with effective leadership and engaged team members. We are building a company that people want to be a part of, and our leadership will be empathetic, accessible, and committed to the success of each team member.

Building an efficient operating environment

Efficiency is at the core of our business. Across our production lines, we prioritize streamlined workflows, cross-training, optimized equipment and innovative technologies to deliver high-quality products promptly while minimizing waste. Combining these with effective communication and employee well-being initiatives not only boosts productivity and profitability but also underscores our commitment to sustainability and customer satisfaction.

Meeting the financial expectations of our stakeholders

In order to accomplish our Vision, the company needs to

perform financially. We will do this by growing sales from new and existing partners while maximizing net income and our cash position, ensuring a positive return for our team and our shareholders.

Values *We believe in dependability, putting in the work, showing respect, and being trustworthy, all while having fun*

Dependability is the cornerstone of effective collaboration, ensuring that every member can be relied upon to fulfill their responsibilities consistently. It fosters trust, cohesion, and productivity within the team, leading to successful outcomes and sustainable growth.

Hard-working individuals possess an unwavering dedication to their tasks, consistently putting in maximum effort to achieve their goals. Their resilience in the face of challenges and commitment to excellence serve as inspiring examples of diligence and determination.

Respect in the workplace is fundamental for fostering a positive and inclusive environment where every individual feels valued and heard. It cultivates a culture of mutual appreciation, understanding, and cooperation, laying the groundwork for productivity and harmonious relationships among team members.

Being trustworthy means consistently demonstrating integrity and reliability in all interactions, earning the confidence and respect of others through honesty and transparency. Trustworthiness forms the bedrock of strong relationships and enables effective collaboration by ensuring that commitments are honored and communication is open and truthful.

The Commerce Platform

This case study describes how Megan applied the PVTV framework within a division of a large, global organization. This team, which we will call The Commerce Platform, demonstrates the scalability of the PVTV approach, showing how it can be leveraged to align a team's PVTV with the overarching company's goal and objectives. This case study provides facilitators and their teams with an inspiring example of integrating PVTV principles to foster innovation, optimize performance, and cultivate a strong, empathetic team culture in a large enterprise setting. By understanding the strategic application of the PVTV methodology, teams can see how to effectively bring their own Visions to life, ensuring seamless and efficient business operations.

Purpose *Our Purpose is to provide an effortless commerce experience*

> We believe this because we want to make working with our Company easy for everyone. Commerce Platform will become the singular company digital experience that provides customers the ability to make easily navigable buying decisions with the confidence that their purchases and usage are secure. Our global capabilities will provide stakeholders the potential to grant access across all product lines in the company around the globe.

Vision *Our Vision is to become the preferred online experience*

240

that seamlessly integrates customers with their products and services, providing unparalleled access and trust in every transaction. We aim to achieve this by. . .

- Providing the most innovative capabilities to our stakeholders to develop, market and sell their products through new methods and opening up new opportunities
- Provide transparency of platform and product health through advanced telemetry and continuous optimization
- Set expectations with cadenced releases of new features that meet evolving customer needs.
- Expanding platform adoption across the organization and enabling the business to discover new ways to generate revenue
- Building and maintaining a strong, empathetic, and transparent team culture.

Tenets *We will do this by . . .*

Keeping the Ship Afloat
We will do this by ensuring platform stability and reliability, reducing tech debt and providing above industry standard performance rates.

Focusing on What Our Customers Need and Solving Their Problems
We will do this by actively listening to our stakeholders, finding the problem they need us to solve and offering a global solution that all our business units can benefit from.

Marketing the Platform Continuously and Using Every Communication Channel

We will do this by ensuring all 15,000 employees know what we are capable of by promoting our platform's benefits and updates across various channels to reach a wider audience.

Celebrating Our Accomplishments Outwardly

We will do this by sharing our successes and milestones within the team, with leadership, and stakeholders to enhance team motivation, increase customer trust, so that we have a positive brand image.

Values

Being Passionate About Delivering a Quality User Experience

We believe in consistently exceeding customer expectations through high-quality interactions and features.

Being Sympathetic to Our Customers' Needs and Empathetic to Our Team

We believe in understanding and addressing the needs and concerns of both our customers and team members. We will do this by fostering open communication, providing support, and creating a collaborative environment.

Transparency + Reliability + Accountability = Trusted

We believe in building trust through honest communication, consistent performance, and taking responsibility for our actions.

Thoughtful and Deliberate Progress and Innovation Globally
We believe in making measured, strategic advancements that drive global innovation and growth.

Liminist

This case study demonstrates how Teresa, the solopreneur behind Liminist, effectively used the PVTV framework to scale her business. Unlike the examples of Jeff's small to medium-sized enterprise or Megan's global team, Teresa's story uniquely showcases a solopreneur leveraging the PVTV principles for substantial growth and impact.

The study highlights Liminist's use of the Flywheel Effect—a cyclical process that continuously aligns and enhances the company's Purpose and Vision. Through this strategic application, Liminist refined its Vision statement to measure and reach its ambitious targets more effectively. This case serves as a model for facilitators and their teams, offering insights on utilizing the Flywheel Effect to stay focused on its Purpose while strategically progressing toward their Vision.

Purpose *To create a world where having a transformative mindset is valued over all other skillsets.*

At Liminist, we champion the transformative mindset as the cornerstone of personal and professional success. We believe that fostering this mindset unlocks unparalleled potential in individuals and teams, making adaptability, innovation, and resilience more attainable. Liminist's approach prioritizes and cultivates transformative thinking as a fundamental skill, preparing our clients to navigate today's dynamic environments and lead with vision and influence. Our methodology integrates rigorous assessments, personalized coaching, and strategic development to replace stagnant practices with dynamic, forward-thinking behaviors. By valuing a transformative mindset above all, we empower clients to redefine boundaries, exceed expectations, and achieve enduring success.

Vision *(Original) To be sought after by leaders and teams that need a perspective transformation and an actionable plan.*

FUN FACT: For Liminist we realized our Vision wasn't specific enough to break down into themes and specific objectives. We would not know if we actually achieved our Vision. So, after this activity, we revised the three-year Vision to read, "To triple Liminist's revenue as leaders' first choice for perspective transformation, with 65% seeking us out for our unique insights."

Liminist recognizes the myriads of coaching solutions available today. We are set apart by our unwavering commitment to challenge conventional thinking and false constructs and go beyond simply advocating a growth mindset. We're dedicated to transforming leadership by dismantling barriers and enhancing strategic perspectives that drive real change in personal and organizational growth.

Success will be measured by establishing differentiated

thought leadership, amplified brand visibility, measurable expansion and impact through direct inquiries, and maintaining a 65% rate from referrals and recognition.

Tenets *We will do this by. . .*

- Being known
- Aligning with the right partners and tools
- Developing impactful proof points
- Staying unique and differentiated

Values *By being. . .*

- Selfless and putting other's successes first,
- Joyful and taking a positive outlook on life and business
- Forgiving
- and Measurable

The Flywheeel Effect
To get the Flywheel spinning, Liminist plans to start with these two Tenets.

> *Being known and aligning with the right partners and tools*
> Position Liminist as a thought leader in transformative leadership and team coaching by completing the following tasks and initiatives.
> - Achieve certifications in The Five Behaviors and Positive Intelligence.
> - Attain paid Vistage speaker approval.
> - Publish *The Purpose Playbook*, a cornerstone of our thought leadership.

- Engage in TEDx training and craft impactful topics.
- Boost LinkedIn thought leadership engagement by over 100% year-over-year.
- Participate in three significant podcasts.
- Accumulate ten new Google Business reviews and LinkedIn recommendations.

If these Tenets are set up correctly, the next two on the list should start spinning.

Developing impactful proof points and staying unique and differentiated
Increase Liminist's brand visibility and recognition in the executive coaching industry.
- Secure keynote speaking opportunities at three major conferences, ideally with Liminist clients.
- Facilitate client nominations for prestigious awards such as the ICF Prism Award and/or ATD Excellence in Practice.
- Launch a second edition of The Purpose Playbook to reinforce Liminist's expertise.
- Enhance Liminist's presence and advocacy on LinkedIn (ideally, clients creating posts talking about Liminist and Teresa).
- Obtain an additional ten Google Business reviews and LinkedIn recommendations.

As all the Tenets start spinning, Liminist should start seeing progress toward its Vision.

Expansion and Impact

Triple Liminist's revenue through direct inquiries, maintaining a 65% rate from referrals and recognition.

- Utilize established thought leadership to organize exclusive Liminist events with over 25 attendees, featuring transformative mindset coaching success stories that align with Liminist's Purpose.
- Secure keynote speaking opportunities at a premier industry event like the TEDx Atlanta, emphasizing the transformative impact of our coaching.
- Achieve an optimal mix of advertising and advocacy to enhance lead generation and inbound responses, maintaining a 65% rate from referrals and recognition.

As you reflect upon this example, consider Liminist's Tenets as stages in a cyclic journey. Starting with "Aligning with the right partners and tools," we set the initial motion that distinguishes Liminist and impacts the market. As the flywheel spins, each Tenet builds upon the last, enhancing Liminist's unique market stance and creating impactful work that retains and attracts clients and fosters advocacy.

This strategic, cyclical process embodies Liminist's Purpose and accelerates our Vision, proving the power of a well-structured strategic approach.

The Flywheeel Effect Checklist
To apply what maximizes each Tenet's contribution to your Vision and Purpose, consider these key areas for your own business:

- ☐ **Organizational Change:** Can you track the adoption of transformational practices introduced by your organization and its impact?

- ☐ **Industry Influence:** Consider monitoring engagement metrics such as views, attendance, and influence on industry trends.
- ☐ **Client Success Stories:** Collect and share case studies and testimonials.
- ☐ **Social Impact:** Document initiatives with non-profits and cultural shifts.
- ☐ **Business Metrics:** Analyze participation and advocacy rates, and professional growth trajectories.

Implementing the Flywheel:

- ☐ **Measurement and Enhancement:** Regularly assess the impact of each Tenet on your Purpose and Vision. For example, evaluate how well "Aligning with the right partners and tools" enhances Liminist's Purpose through improved partnership and tool utilization metrics.
- ☐ **Strategic Adjustments:** Use insights gained to fine-tune or introduce new initiatives that better support the Vision and Purpose.
- ☐ **Continuous Improvement Loop:** Establish a feedback mechanism using the Vision and Purpose statements to refine your Tenets continually, ensuring each cycle of the Flywheel achieves and amplifies your strategic objectives.

By following these steps, inspired by Liminist's practice, you can bring your Vision to life strategically and effectively.

GLOSSARY

THE PURPOSE PLAYBOOK TERMINOLOGY

Critical Number: The beating heart of *The Great Game,* rallying the team around a unifying goal that defines winning and blending ownership mindset with strategic insight, all encompassed within a dynamic trio of knowing, tracking, and sharing. The Critical Number is a metric that represents a weakness or vulnerability that could negatively impact a business's performance and long-term security. This is the focus of measuring your PVTV year over year until you've reached your Vision.

Flywheel Effect: Represents sustained momentum in business, as highlighted by Jim Collins in his book, *Good to Great.* This principle propels teams toward ever-increasing successes through consistent, strategic efforts. Like a massive wheel gaining speed with each push, the Flywheel Effect embodies the cumulative impact principle, where initial hard work yields greater ease and acceleration over time. Essential for advancing your PVTV, it harnesses collective actions that build upon one another, driving closer to your Vision with each cycle.

Key Performance Indicators (KPIs): Referred to in the Turnaround Universe as "Areas of Focus," KPIs are scorecards for your performance tied to important business goals and objectives. The Critical Number shines as the most crucial KPI, showcasing what matters most. These are defined for each quarter in the year to achieve your Critical Number.

Metrics: Act as success yardsticks, giving you a read on how you're doing or how much ground you're covering accomplishing your KPIs, which in turn help you hit your annual Critical Number. Think of them as tools to fine-tune and improve specific tactics and strategies.

Purpose: Encapsulates the fundamental core essence of your company's (or team's) existence, guiding its behavior, shaping how it acts, and impacting everyone it serves.

Purpose Index: A numerical gauge that measures how faithfully a company sticks to its Purpose Statement. Think of it as a compass that keeps your company's actions and decisions aligned with its core Purpose. It's a way to check, quantitatively, whether the team is living up to the ideals set out in the Purpose Statement, ensuring the company's journey stays true to its foundational essence over time.

Team: The word team is used often in this book. It can represent a Company, Business Unit, Department, or group of people aligned to the same objectives.

Tenets: Well-thought-out moves you work on to secure that major victory aligned with your Vision. If we were diving into business jargon, you might call them "Strategies" or "Approaches."

Values: Soul-deep beliefs and top priorities that guide how someone or a group behaves. Imagine them as an inner compass of principles steering both personal and organizational choices.

Vision: Paints a picture of where your organization dreams to be in the next three to five years – it's all about your big goal and the roadmap you're crafting for the future.

FINAL THOUGHTS

REFLECTING ON THE JOURNEY

As you close the pages of *The Purpose Playbook*, remember that the journey you've embarked upon is both transformational and ongoing. Embracing PVTV is about creating a strategy and nurturing a living, breathing ethos that resonates through every aspect of your leadership and organization. The steps you've taken and the insights you've gained here are just the beginning. Carry them forward with conviction and passion. Remember, the true power of *The Purpose Playbook* and all its activities lies in its conception, daily practice, and evolution.

May your Purpose-driven journey be as fulfilling as it is successful. Keep evolving, keep inspiring, and let your Purpose light the way.

You're Done! Yet, are you really done?

We are so excited you successfully reached the end of this Playbook. Well done! Congratulations!

You are not really done, though . . . In the fast-paced world of business, staying ahead means continually evolving and adapting. Your journey as a leader (and team member) is never truly complete. To keep your organization thriving, it's essential to review this Playbook annually and re-envision your Vision Statement every three to five years.

To kick off this ongoing process, Jeff, Megan, and Teresa have compiled a checklist to help you confirm that your organization has addressed all the key elements listed in the Playbook.

Playbook Completion Checklist

Purpose, Vision, Values, & Tenets

☐ **Define Your Purpose:** Your Purpose is the core reason your organization exists. It should be ambitious, nearly unattainable, yet compelling enough to drive your team forward. Example: "Our Purpose is to drive the global transition to sustainable energy."

☐ **Craft a Clear Vision:** Vision statements should paint a picture of where your organization aims to be in the next three to five years. It should be aspirational yet grounded in reality, guiding your strategic decisions. Example: "Our Vision is to become the leading provider of innovative eco-friendly energy solutions by 2030."

☐ **Develop Tenets:** These are the strategic pillars that will help you achieve your Vision and fulfill your Purpose. Tenets should be specific, measurable, and directly tied to your overall goals.

☐ **Identify Core Values:** Values are the principles that guide your team's behavior and decision-making. Ensure they are clear, actionable, and embody the culture you want to cultivate.

Implementation and Operationalization

- ☐ **Align Daily Actions with PVTV:** Your Purpose, Vision, Tenets, & Values (PVTV) should be integrated into every aspect of your organization's operations. This includes starting meetings by reciting the PVTV and ensuring all team activities align with these foundational elements.
- ☐ **Monitor and Adjust:** Regularly review your PVTV with your team to ensure it remains relevant and effective. Adjust as necessary to stay aligned with your evolving objectives and external changes.

Team Engagement and Development

- ☐ **Collaborate on PVTV Creation:** Engage your team in the development of the PVTV to foster ownership and commitment. Use exercises like Vision collages and Value mapping to gather diverse perspectives and build a unified strategy.
- ☐ **Embrace Failure as Growth:** Cultivate a culture where failure is seen as an opportunity to learn and improve. Use structured activities to analyze failures and develop actionable plans to prevent recurrence and drive continuous improvement.

Strategic Planning and Execution

- ☐ **Set Clear Objectives and Milestones:** Break down your Vision into achievable milestones and actionable steps. Ensure each team member understands their role in achieving these objectives.
- ☐ **Foster Continuous Improvement:** Encourage ongoing

evaluation and refinement of your strategies and processes. Use feedback and performance metrics to guide your adjustments and enhance overall effectiveness.

Leadership and Culture

- ☐ **Lead by Example:** Demonstrate commitment to the PVTV through your actions and decisions. Your leadership sets the tone for the entire organization.
- ☐ **Promote Open Communication:** Facilitate open dialogue about the PVTV, encouraging team members to share their thoughts and feedback. This openness helps maintain alignment and fosters a sense of belonging and Purpose.

These key takeaways and reminders serve as a practical guide to ensure your organization remains focused, aligned, and driven by its Purpose, Vision, Tenets, & Values. By embedding these elements into your daily operations and strategic planning, you can navigate challenges effectively and achieve sustained success.

Still need help?

As with many Playbooks, they are a great first start. Yet, sometimes, it helps to have an expert come in and facilitate these discussions. We are here to help!

Just go to **AlwaysLeadWithPurpose.com** to learn how to reach us.

ABOUT THE AUTHORS

Jeff Hilimire is the bestselling author of the Turnaround Leadership Series and an accomplished entrepreneur who has launched multiple organizations and successfully sold two companies. He is currently a Partner at Purpose Group, a purpose-driven holding company focused on bringing PVTV to organizations across the United States. He is currently the Board Chair at Dragon Army, an award-winning digital engagement company, as well as the founder of Ripples Media.

Hilimire is also the co-founder and board member of two nonprofit organizations. 48in48 is a global nonprofit that produces hackathon events, building 48 nonprofit websites in 48 hours. The A Pledge creates a path for systemic opportunity in Atlanta by inspiring marketing and advertising agencies to commit to matching the diversity of their team to that of our city by 2030.

Jeff lives in Atlanta with his wife Emily and their five children. You can follow Jeff's adventures on his personal blog, jeffhilimire. com, or sign up for his newsletter at jeffhilimire.com/newsletter.

Teresa Caro Teresa Caro is the founder and CEO of Liminist, where she leverages her unique leadership approach to drive growth and enhance performance in C-suite executives, senior leaders, and high-potential teams.

As an ICF credentialed executive and teams coach, Teresa empowers individuals and teams to achieve excellence, adaptability, and strategic impact. She is an Authorized Partner for The Five Behaviors® by Wiley, PXT Select certified, and a Positive Intelligence Coach, enabling her to foster a transformative mindset in her clients.

With over two decades of leadership in high-stakes environments, Teresa has guided leadership teams and marketing departments toward significant achievements. Her expertise covers sectors like CPG, Retail, Fintech, and B2B SaaS.

An avid golfer, yoga enthusiast, and a person who cherishes family time, Teresa believes in the power of strategic prioritization, encouraging her clients to focus on what's most important at each stage of their personal and professional journeys.

You can find Teresa at TheLiminist.com.

Megan Barney is a seasoned technology executive with extensive experience bridging IT delivery and product management in global enterprises. She excels in optimizing software development frameworks, fostering stakeholder collaboration, and cultivating high-performing teams. Megan drives strategic growth by aligning technical solutions with business objectives to create innovative products, while also leading initiatives that promote a positive and inclusive technology community.

Her leadership style is characterized by a focus on empowering teams, leveraging company values to create a motivated and cohesive workplace. Megan's work in optimizing development frameworks and streamlining complex business processes has consistently delivered measurable results, positioning her as a trusted leader in the technology space.

In addition to her professional accomplishments, Megan is involved in the broader tech community. She has chaired company affinity groups, developed an annual company-wide technology summit, and served as a society board member within Georgia's technology association (TAG), reflecting her dedication to fostering a positive and inclusive environment both within and beyond her organization.

ACKNOWLEDGEMENTS

First, a note from all three authors. . .

We want to extend our heartfelt thanks to Ripples Media for your exceptional support in bringing *The Purpose Playbook* to life. Managing three authors was no small task, yet your joy and expertise made the process surprisingly smooth. Your skill in visualizing and organizing *The Purpose Playbook* has ensured that it is both easy to read and practical to use. Thank you for being an invaluable partner in this journey.

Jeff

I am honored to have had the chance to write a book with Teresa Caro and Megan Barney. They are two of the smartest, most passionate people I've ever had a chance to work with, and they have taken *The Purpose Playbook* to places I didn't even know were possible.

I'd also like to thank all the great teams I've had a chance to work with that helped infuse this book coming together, including, but not limited to: the OG team at Spunlogic, Engauge, Dragon Army, Ripples Media, 48in48, The A Pledge, and our Purpose Group companies, Gerald Printing / Liberty Imaging and Alloy.

And I always have to thank my family, the 7mires, for supporting me as I lock myself away to write these books.

Teresa

Writing this book has been a wonderful journey, one made possible by a host of incredible people who have supported and inspired me along the way.

To my parents and siblings, thank you for always being there, cheering me on, and instilling the values and confidence that have guided me through life. Your support has made me who I am today, and I love who I am!

A special shoutout to my husband, Dave, and our daughter, Ace. You have always encouraged me to think differently and pushed my perspectives further. Ace, I especially appreciate you enduring my endless ideas with minimal eye-rolling—your patience means the world to me.

Big thanks to Jeff for being an important figure in my life and for your partnership in crystallizing my thoughts on teamwork. Working with you in different ways through the decades has transformed these insights into something truly actionable.

To Megan, thank you for trusting me as your co-author, coach, and friend. Our connection has brought immense joy to my life.

A nod to Patrick Lencioni, Brené Brown, and Scott Galloway – your work on vulnerability and trust in business has deeply influenced my approach and this book. I now trust the word "Trust!"

I'm profoundly grateful to each of you for your part in this endeavor. Writing this book has been both a challenge and a fulfilling experience—thank you.

Megan

Writing a book was beyond my wildest dreams; usually, I just (politely) scream my passions to anyone who will listen. To be able to take exercises out of my PowerPoint deck and curate them to share with the public brings me immense joy. I want to thank some of the folks who helped me get here…

To my husband, Michael Barney, for supporting my ambitions and reminding me when it's time to log off.

To my Dad, Kevin Hickey, for always listening while I carried on incessantly about how I wanted to change the way teams operate.

To the various teams at Equifax, for being my "proving ground" and letting me test many of the exercises in this book.

To Jeff Hilimire, for your trust in me as a co-author in your Turnaround Literary Universe.

To Teresa Caro, for being an extraordinary writing partner and coach as I continue to evolve my own leadership journey.

I am truly thankful to everyone who has journeyed alongside me through various chapters of my life and career. Your lessons and influence have propelled me in a direction I never imagined possible.

OTHER TITLES FROM THE
TURNAROUND LITERARY UNIVERSE

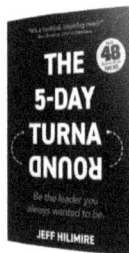

The 5-Day Turnaround

Learn how to grow your business or team by leading like an entrepreneur. This book will help you embrace a startup mentality to create transformative growth.

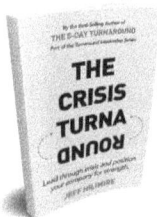

The Crisis Turnaround

Leading a successful business is hard enough, and it's even harder during an emergency. This book will help you thrive even in times of crisis, and become stronger as a result.

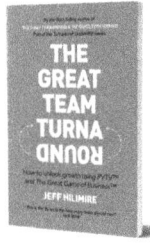

The Great Team Turnaround

Can a shared Purpose unlock your organization's best work? Using insights from PVTV and *The Great Game of Business,* this book will enable teams to reach their full potential.

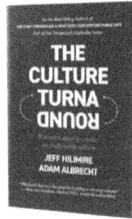

The Culture Turnaround

Culture is routinely cited as one of the main reasons organizations find success. But what is an *undeniable* culture? This book will help you jumpstart growth in the face of competition and other obstacles.

9 798991 387019